# Making
# CONNECTIONS

**3**

## Skills and Strategies for Academic Reading

### Third Edition

# Teacher's Manual

Kenneth J. Pakenham | Jo McEntire | Jessica Williams

CAMBRIDGE
UNIVERSITY PRESS

# CAMBRIDGE
## UNIVERSITY PRESS

32 Avenue of the Americas, New York NY 10013-2473, USA

Cambridge University Press is part of the University of Cambridge.

It furthers the University's mission by disseminating knowledge in the pursuit of education, learning and research at the highest international levels of excellence.

www.cambridge.org
Information on this title: www.cambridge.org/9781107650541

First published 2005
Second edition 2013
3rd printing 2014

*A catalogue record for this publication is available from the British Library*

ISBN  978-1-107-67301-4  Student's Book
ISBN  978-1-107-65054-1  Teacher's Manual

Cambridge University Press has no responsibility for the persistence or accuracy of URLs for external or third-party internet websites referred to in this publication, and does not guarantee that any content on such websites is, or will remain, accurate or appropriate.

Layout services and book design: Page Designs International, Inc.
Cover design: Studio Montage

# Contents

# Teaching Suggestions

The *Making Connections 3* Student's Book consists of four units, each of which is organized in the following way:

- Three Skills and Strategies sections alternate with the readings. The first precedes Readings 1 and 2, the second precedes Readings 3 and 4, and the third precedes Reading 5. These sections introduce and practice specific skills and strategies for reading.
- Five readings are each accompanied by associated activities in reading and vocabulary development. The fifth reading is the longest, and offers students a reading experience similar to the challenges of the reading assignments they will meet in their future academic studies.
- A final section, Making Connections, provides two cohesion-building exercises.

High-intermediate–level students and above need to expand their vocabulary in order to prepare for academic courses. Strategies and activities to help students expand their vocabulary are therefore important features of *Making Connections 3*. The post-reading activities following each of the four readings in a unit include tasks that facilitate vocabulary expansion by focusing on 20–25 vocabulary items used in the reading. Additionally, tasks for vocabulary from the Academic Word List (AWL) follow the second, fourth, and fifth readings. All vocabulary items are listed and defined, with an example provided, in Appendix 1 of the Student's Book (pages 256–270). In Appendix 2 of the Student's Book (pages 271–272), each key vocabulary item is indexed by the unit and the reading in which it is first used. The ⒶⒷ icon indicates vocabulary items from the AWL.

*Making Connections 3* has enough material for a reading course of 50 to 70 class hours, assuming a corresponding number of hours are available for homework assignments. Completing all the Beyond the Reading activities that accompany each reading might make the course longer.

Skills, strategies, and vocabulary are recycled within a unit and in subsequent units. It is recommended, therefore, that in planning a course outline, the order of the book be followed.

## Skills and Strategies

The Skills and Strategies sections introduce strategies to teach comprehension in reading, vocabulary building, and understanding of grammatical structures in text. These strategies are then incorporated into the reading activities.

### Rationale

Research suggests that good readers apply various strategies when they are reading a text. The Skills and Strategies sections introduce and provide practice with a variety of these reading strategies.

### Description

The first two Skills and Strategies sections of each unit focus on text comprehension skills and strategies: identifying main ideas, cause and effect, continuing ideas, point of view, identifying main ideas of a text, definition and clarification, problem-solution texts, and graphic material. The third Skills and Strategies section in each unit focuses on language – specifically, the understanding of lexicon and grammatical structures: managing unknown vocabulary, reduced relative clauses, passive sentences, and nominalization in subjects.

Each Skills and Strategies section provides Skill Practice activities that move students from recognition to production. More practice is provided in the While You Read section. Students then review each skill and strategy within the Skill Review section. Strategies are recycled throughout the text.

### How to Use

The Skills and Strategies sections are best introduced in class, supported by the use of other materials (e.g., examples similar to those in the Examples & Explanations subsection). At the beginning of the course, each of the Skill Practice activities should be partially completed in class. Then, when you are confident that your students understand the form and content of each activity, an appropriate number of items can be assigned for homework.

# Before You Read

## Connecting to the Topic

### Rationale

The purpose of this activity is to get students to activate background knowledge relevant to the content of the reading that follows. Effective reading occurs when readers are able to place new information within the context of information they already possess.

### Description

This is the first of two activities that occur before each reading. It consists of questions for discussion with a partner.

### How to Use

This activity can be introduced through short, full-class discussions. Partners or small groups can then continue the discussions.

## Previewing and Predicting

### Rationale

The purpose of this activity is to get students into the habit of previewing the content and organization of a text before they start reading in depth. Previewing has been shown to be a key strategy that enhances a reader's ability to understand a text on first encounter.

### Description

*Making Connections 3* uses different techniques for previewing texts. Students are taught to look at titles, headings, pictures, and graphic information such as charts to guess what information might appear, or to form questions that they expect a reading to answer. Each technique encourages the student to interact with the text before beginning to read for deeper understanding.

### How to Use

These activities are best introduced, modeled, and practiced in class. We recommend that students first work with a partner. The primary goal of this activity is to encourage active interaction with the text.

# While You Read

## Rationale

Research suggests that good readers read actively by asking themselves questions and monitoring comprehension as they read. The While You Read tasks encourage students to adopt this approach. These tasks focus students' attention on the strategic nature of the reading process during their first read-through of a text. These tasks appear in the margins of the text and force students to stop and apply the strategies presented in the earlier Skills and Strategies sections. Students are thus encouraged to do what good readers do – to interact with the text while they read.

## Description

While You Read boxes are in the margin of every reading, opposite some words in bold blue within a line of text. Students are directed to stop reading at the end of the sentence containing the bold blue text and to perform a strategic task designed to support effective reading.

While You Read provides practice for the skills and strategies previously introduced. It provides practice in text comprehension by having students identify main ideas and supporting details, point of view, and understand connections between paragraphs. It reinforces lexical and grammatical skills by having students identify context clues to meaning, and demonstrate understanding of reduced relative clauses, passive sentences, and nominalization in subjects.

## How to Use

While You Read is best introduced and modeled as a classroom activity after the reading has been previewed. We recommend that you first introduce students to the concept of active reading. You can do this by reading the first few paragraphs of the first reading of Unit 1 out loud. As you come to each bold blue word, stop and read the While You Read directions. Answer the question before you continue to read. Note that this technique will be new to many students, particularly those who do not read extensively in their own language. Students will find it a time-consuming process at first, but assure them that, with practice, they will gradually apply these strategies automatically and their reading speed and comprehension will increase.

At first, many of the boxes in the shorter readings can be completed during an initial in-class read-through. This will allow you to provide students with the intensive guidance, practice, and immediate feedback on their performances that they will need as they learn to apply these skills independently.

To help students focus on the reading process, it is strongly recommended that no dictionary be used during this first read-through. We also recommend that the first read-through include reading for main ideas. (See the Main Idea Check section below.)

One challenge in the While You Read activity is that students tend to make excessive use of highlighting and/or underlining. Try to help students understand that highlighting or underlining entire paragraphs, for example, is not an effective reading strategy. In fact, indiscriminate highlighting is a counterproductive activity. To avoid this, have the students follow the directions provided in the Skills and Strategies sections: highlight main ideas only, number supporting details, and underline key vocabulary.

# Reading Skill Development

## Main Idea Check

### Rationale

Students often focus too much on the details in a reading rather than on its main ideas. The Main Idea Check activity provides an opportunity for students to focus on an understanding of the main ideas of each paragraph. It is only after students have grasped the main ideas of a reading that they can make sense of how the details fit into this larger frame of meaning.

### Description

The Main Idea Check has students identify the main idea of different paragraphs by matching the paragraph number to the sentence expressing its main idea.

### How to Use

After you work through the strategy-based approach to main idea identification in Skills and Strategies 1, Unit 1, the Main Idea Check tasks may be assigned for work in class or for homework. In classes with additional writing goals, students could be asked to rewrite the sentences of the Main Idea Check tasks in their own words and then put the sentences together to form a summary of the given reading.

## A Closer Look

### Rationale

Having understood the main ideas in a reading, students need to achieve a more in-depth understanding of it. In this activity, therefore, students are asked to go back to the reading and read for details and to establish connections among them.

### Description

Many of the questions in A Closer Look are types of questions with which students will probably be familiar (e.g., true/false and multiple choice). We recommend that early on in the text, you review some common strategies in answering multiple-choice questions. You can encourage students to use the following strategies:

- Read the directions very carefully.
- Read all the possible answers before choosing the correct one.
- Eliminate the obviously incorrect answers.
- Recognize that a wrong answer may include an incorrect fact or information not in the reading.
- Recognize that all information within the answer must be true for the answer to be correct.

You should also alert students to one question type that is possibly less familiar. To encourage the synthesizing of information, a significant number of multiple-choice questions have more than one correct answer. This question type is introduced by the directions, *Circle all that apply*.

### How to Use

Generally, the tasks in A Closer Look lend themselves well to completion outside of class. However, we suggest that at first you give students some classroom practice in answering this section.

A useful tool for students as they complete A Closer Look tasks is Appendix 1, Key Vocabulary (pages 256–270 in the Student's Book). This appendix lists the vocabulary alphabetically within each reading, thus providing accessible and convenient support for students during these more detailed examinations of the readings. For more information on Appendix 1, see page 7 of this Teacher's Manual.

## Skill Review

### Rationale

Students need multiple opportunities to practice new reading and vocabulary-building skills and strategies. This is particularly important as new skills are introduced that build upon understanding of those previously taught.

### Description

The Skill Review allows students to practice specific skills introduced in the Skills and Strategies sections. The content reflects the previous reading, and therefore should be sufficiently familiar to enable students to focus on the skill itself.

### How to Use

This is a good homework assignment. Students can then compare their work in small groups. If students encounter problems with this task, direct them back to the appropriate Skills and Strategies section. It is worth taking the time in class to really explain these tasks since they are key to academic reading.

# Vocabulary Development

## Definitions

### Rationale

This activity provides structured way for students to begin to learn the target vocabulary in each of the 20 readings.

### Description

In this activity, students find a word in the reading that is similar in meaning to each of 10–15 dictionary-style definitions. This is a simple way for students to focus on target vocabulary in context without having to use bilingual dictionaries. Part-of-speech information about the target vocabulary has been provided so that students can integrate this information into the vocabulary-learning process.

### How to Use

This activity is best introduced as a classroom activity. It can then be completed either in or out of class as homework.

## Words in Context

### Rationale

Understanding the meaning of unknown target words by perceiving the surrounding context of the word has been demonstrated to be an important skill in vocabulary acquisition. This activity helps students to see the linguistic contexts in which the target words belong.

### Description

There are three types of Words in Context activities: fill-in-the-blank within sentences, fill-in-the blanks within paragraphs, and matching. All activities introduce words or phrases from the readings that have not been targeted in the preceding Definitions exercise. The key vocabulary items are presented at the beginning of the activity.

### How to Use

This activity can be completed either in or out of class. Encourage students to go back to the reading and find the target words if they cannot readily answer the questions. Although these words are recycled in later readings, we encourage you to expand this practice by creating vocabulary tests focusing on these target words. Testing students on some of the vocabulary from Unit 1 while they are working on later units, for example, will help them to retain vocabulary.

## Synonyms

### Rationale

Students need multiple ways to learn key vocabulary. The Synonyms activity offers the chance to focus on the meaning of key words by connecting that meaning to familiar words and phrases.

### Description

Each item in the activity requires students to select the correct target vocabulary word or phrase that is closest in meaning to the words in parentheses. Students then use this information to fill in the blank lines for each sentence.

### How to Use

This activity is appropriate for both in and out of class work.

# Word Families

## Rationale

High-intermediate learners need to build their academic vocabulary quickly in order to be successful in more advanced courses. Recognizing different word forms allows students to increase their receptive vocabulary quickly and efficiently. By focusing on parts of speech, this approach to vocabulary building also may help students move toward the ability to use the vocabulary in writing and speech.

## Description

This activity is introduced after the second reading of each unit. It introduces five word families. The boldface word in each family is the part of speech that appears in the reading. Students are instructed to locate the words in the reading and use context clues to figure out the meanings. If the students are still unsure, you may direct them to Appendix 1 on pages 256–270 to check the meaning of unfamiliar vocabulary. Students choose the correct word form to complete the 10 fill-in-the-blank sentences.

## How to Use

We recommend that you introduce this activity in class, as students may need more instruction in parts of speech. They may also need guidance in using the correct form of the word.

# Academic Word List

## Rationale

The Academic Word List (Coxhead, 2000) provides a corpus of the most frequently used academic words. *Making Connections 3* provides students with the opportunity to learn this vocabulary, an activity key to preparing for academic coursework in all fields of study.

## Description

After the second and fourth readings, this fill-in-the-sentence activity focuses on AWL vocabulary items from the two preceding readings. The AWL activity after the fifth reading provides an opportunity to review academic vocabulary items from the entire unit.

## How to Use

Before you begin this activity, it is important to explain the significance of general academic vocabulary. Make sure that students know AWL items are not technical, subject-specific terms but rather general words common to all academic coursework. Research has shown that students need familiarity with this vocabulary in order to understand college texts.

The Academic Word List activity provides an opportunity for students to go back to the readings and explore vocabulary if needed. This can be done out of class, but it also works well as a group activity with students discussing possible answers and referring to the readings to explain their choices. It is recommended that students learn this vocabulary by making word cards.

# Same or Different

## Rational

This activity performs several important functions. It provides further opportunities for students to work with the vocabulary they have encountered throughout the unit; it develops their skill for recognizing paraphrasing; and it helps move students away from a word-centered approach to reading.

## Description

This activity follows the Academic Word activity in the fifth reading. The task consists of pairs of sentences that incorporate vocabulary from the entire unit. Students are asked to decide on the semantic equivalence of the two sentences in each pair.

## How to Use

Same or Different is a good group activity since it provokes discussion about the meanings of individual words and sentences. Direct students to focus on the meaning of the introductory sentence. Then have them consider whether the elements in the following sentences are compatible or incompatible with that sentence.

# Beyond the Reading

## Critical Thinking

### Rationale

A successful college student does not merely accumulate information. Rather, that student engages in thoughtful, reflective, and independent thinking in order to make sense of a text. Critical thinking skills enable a student to evaluate what they read, make connections, ask questions, solve problems, and apply that information to new situations.

### Description

Each Critical Thinking activity defines a specific critical thinking skill, and then allows students to practice that skill in a context linked to the previous reading. Examples of specific skills include clarifying concepts, applying information to new situations, and offering opinions.

### How to Use

Before you begin this activity, it is a good idea to discuss the difference between memorization and comprehension. Introduce critical thinking skills as an essential part of comprehension. This is particularly important as some students may come from educational systems that emphasize rote learning rather than critical thinking. The activity itself could be assigned to in-class groups or as homework. The latter would allow a student to spend time exploring the specific critical thinking skill. Students could then compare their responses in groups.

## Research

### Rationale

Some teachers may want to use the readings as an opportunity for their students to undertake some research on the topics of the readings.

### Description

This activity occurs after each of the 20 readings. It offers topics for students to research and discuss that are relevant to the subject of a reading.

### How to Use

The research questions offer opportunities for students to tackle more challenging reading tasks as well as to pursue more personally stimulating aspects of a given topic. Some of the research requires students to do self-reflection or survey classmates to gather more data. Some requires students to go online to find additional information.

## Writing

### Rationale

Students develop deeper understanding of a reading and become more adept in using new vocabulary if provided an opportunity to reflect and write about what they have read.

### Description

This writing activity appears at the close of each reading. It allows students to use their discussion and research activity as the basis to write paragraphs.

### How to Use

The paragraphs can be produced in or outside of class. Remind students to use information from their research activity within their writing. It is also a good idea to encourage them to use new vocabulary they have learned from that unit.

## Improving Your Reading Speed

### Rationale

Slow reading is a common complaint of second-language learners. It is frustrating, and it impedes comprehension. While individuals will read at different rates, gradually increasing rates for all students will allow students to read more effectively and with more pleasure and confidence.

### Description

This activity appears at the end of each second and fourth reading. Students are directed to choose one of the previous readings within the unit and time themselves as they read. They then record their time in a chart in Appendix 3 on pages 274–275. This practice provides the opportunity for students to see their reading speed improve as they practice.

### How to Use

We do not recommend that teachers suggest an ideal words-per-minute reading rate for two reasons. First, students will read at different rates. Equally important, good readers vary their rate according to a text and reading purpose. Instead, focus on improving individual rates while stressing that effective reading involves both adequate speed and comprehension.

Have students read Appendix 3 before they complete this activity. This will allow them to learn and practice strategies that will improve their reading rates. It is also important that students identify personal reading habits, such as reading out loud or looking at each individual word, that slow down reading rates.

It is a good idea to complete this activity in class the first time. You might need to help students compute their words-per-minute rates and enter these in their charts. Most of all, stress that like any skill, improving reading speed requires practice.

# Making Connections

As the final review activity of each unit, two exercises give students practice in establishing within short texts the cohesion of vocabulary, structural features, and organizational patterns.

## Rationale

These tasks provide students with a focused opportunity to practice reading for cohesion between sentences and short paragraphs. In addition, students get a further opportunity to review recently targeted academic vocabulary.

## Description

This activity introduces and gives students practice with strategies writers use to achieve cohesion:

- Use of result and response connectors
- Use of correction to previously stated views and cause connectors
- Use of result and contrast connectors
- Use of result and solution connectors

Practice begins at the sentence level and progresses to short paragraphs. Target vocabulary from the unit is recycled throughout this Making Connections section.

## How to Use

This section is probably best performed in class, where fairly immediate feedback is available. Students can work individually or in pairs. Feedback may be supplied by

you and/or elicited from students. You can expand this practice by presenting other jigsaw-type activities. For example, take a paragraph that uses the same cohesion-building strategies.

# Appendices

## Appendix 1: Key Vocabulary
**(pages 256–270)**

Appendix 1 is the "dictionary" for *Making Connections 3*. For each reading, the target vocabulary items are listed alphabetically, defined simply and clearly, and exemplified in a sentence. The dictionary's purpose is to offer students easy access to information on the meaning and use of each word during the vocabulary learning process, especially while they are completing the Vocabulary Development activities. It can also be used during students' work on A Closer Look. Note that vocabulary from the AWL is indicated by the ❹ icon.

## Appendix 2: Index To Key Vocabulary
**(pages 271–272)**

Appendix 2 is an index that lists each key vocabulary item by the unit and the reading in which it is first introduced, thus allowing students to locate the original dictionary entry for a vocabulary item when necessary.

Note that vocabulary from the AWL is indicated by the ❹ icon.

## Appendix 3: Improving Your Reading Speed **(pages 273–275)**

Appendix 3 begins with a list of strategies students can employ in order to improve their reading speed. It is a good idea to discuss these strategies before students practice this skill. It also includes a chart that students will use to record their reading rates as they work through the Student's Book.

# Answer Key

# 1 Global Health

## Skills and Strategies 1
Identifying Main Ideas

### Skill Practice 1 *Page 3*

1. This huge growth has raised many important questions about mental health; b
2. In many cases, heart surgery is lifesaving. However, this practice also raises important medical issues; c
3. infectious diseases such as measles, whooping cough, and simple diarrhea. Emphasizing the prevention rather than the treatment of these diseases could reduce the number of deaths; d

### Skill Practice 2 *Page 4*

1. One reason is that surgery is very expensive, even for rich nations.
   In addition, even where resources for surgical treatment are available, this type of treatment is not always successful for all patients.
2. In 1985, the World Health Organization (WHO) worked to end this disease in North, South, and Central America.
   In 1991, nearly 2 million children in Peru were vaccinated just one week after polio was diagnosed in a two-year old boy.
   The government there [India] partnered with WHO and began regular National Vaccination Days that aimed to vaccinate 170 million children under the age of five.

## Reading 1
The State of the World's Health

### Connecting to the Topic *Page 6*

Answers will vary.

## Previewing and Predicting *Page 6*

| PARAGRAPH | QUESTION |
|---|---|
| 5 | How does the way you live affect your life expectancy? |
| 2 | What is meant by the term *life expectancy*? |
| 6 | How healthy is the world today? |
| 1 | Why is it important for all people to think carefully about their health? |
| 4 | What are some of the causes of premature death? |
| 3 | What is the connection between mortality rates and world health? |

## While You Read *Page 6*

1. life expectancy
2. most countries have seen a significant increase in life expectancy
3. Therefore, although there are reasons to be hopeful about mortality rates worldwide, there are still areas of concern.
4. Severe obesity can reduce life expectancy by as much as 20 years; Smoking is another lifestyle choice that has serious health consequences; Every year, six million people die from tobacco-related products, including those who contract diseases from second-hand smoke

## Reading Skill Development

### Main Idea Check *Page 10*

A 5          D 3
B 2          E 6
C 4

### A Closer Look *Page 10*

1. c          4. c
2. d          5. False
3. b          6. d

## Skill Review *Page 11*

| PARA-GRAPH | FIRST SEN-TENCE | SECOND SEN-TENCE | WHOLE PARA-GRAPH | REPEATED AT THE END OF THE PARA-GRAPH |
|---|---|---|---|---|
| 2 | | | ✓ | ✓ |
| 3 | | | ✓ | ✓ |
| 4 | | ✓ | | |
| 5 | ✓ | | | |
| 6 | | | ✓ | |

# Vocabulary Development

## Definitions *Page 12*

1. indicator
2. assess
3. counterpart
4. optimistic
5. trend
6. target
7. eradicate
8. stigma
9. obesity
10. address

## Words in Context *Page 12*

1. contracted
2. statistics
3. promising
4. considerable
5. correlation
6. monitored
7. devastating
8. virtually
9. accounts for
10. disparities

# Reading 2
## Changing Attitudes Toward Cardiovascular Disease

## Connecting to the Topic *Page 14*

Answers will vary.

## Previewing and Predicting *Page 14*

| PARAGRAPH | TOPIC |
|---|---|
| 7 | Promising results in many countries from changes in attitudes |
| 1 | Connection between daily lives and cardiovascular diseases |
| 5 | Negative news about CVD |
| 3 | Positive effects from changes in attitude |
| 2 | Behavioral changes and CVD |
| 6 | Government attempts to decrease CVD |
| 4 | Better medical understanding and treatment |

## While You Read *Page 14*

1. Many people are no longer relying on doctors for advice and treatment; A greater understanding of the connection between diet and health has led many to reduce or even eliminate food high in fat and cholesterol from their diets. An increasing number of people understand that regular and frequent cardiovascular exercise like walking, running, and swimming reduces stress
2. Deaths from CVD first began to fall in western countries in the 1960s, and this trend continues today.
3. However, little doubt remains that a global strategy to fight CVD is necessary since the disease still accounts for more deaths than any other disease.

# Reading Skill Development

## Main Idea Check *Page 17*

A 3
B 6
C 4
D 2
E 5

## A Closer Look *Page 17*

1. True
2. c
3. True
4. b
5. d
6. b
7. b
8. False

## Skill Review *Page 18*

In the middle of the twentieth century, medical research showed that there was a clear association between cardiovascular disease, or CVD – which includes heart disease, high blood pressure, and stroke – and four factors in people's daily lives: smoking, stress, poor nutrition, and insufficient physical exercise. This awareness initiated a shift in attitudes toward health care. Health experts began to emphasize the idea that everyone can reduce their own chance of having CVD by paying more attention to these four factors. People listened. As a result, many more people now recognize the correlation between a healthy – or unhealthy – heart and lifestyle.

c

# Vocabulary Development

## Definitions *Page 19*

1. stroke
2. shift
3. emphasize
4. demonstrate
5. eliminate
6. cholesterol
7. conduct
8. detection
9. accessible
10. prevalent
11. project
12. collaborate
13. switch
14. link
15. strategy

## Words in Context *Page 19*

1. a  diagnosis
   b  Advances
   c  initiates
   d  effective
2. e  outcome
   f  preventive
   g  aimed at
   h  awareness
   i  aerobic
   j  key

## Academic Word List *Page 20*

1. correlation
2. target
3. considerable
4. accessible
5. strategy
6. monitors
7. indicator
8. detected
9. shift
10. emphasize

# Skills and Strategies 2
## Cause and Effect

### Skill Practice 1 *Page 24*

2. A <u>recent drop in hospital visits</u> is being (blamed on) the
   <u>high cost of healthcare</u>.
   *E ... ← ... C*

3. <u>Air pollution</u> (contributes to) many <u>respiratory diseases,</u>
   <u>such as lung cancer and asthma.</u>
   *C ... → ... E*

4. The police have identified a number of factors that
   (contribute to) <u>traffic accidents,</u> including <u>alcohol,</u>
   <u>speeding, and weather.</u>
   *← ... E ... C*

5. The <u>spring rain</u> (has produced) a <u>record number of</u>
   <u>mosquitoes that carry dangerous diseases.</u>
   *C ... → ... E*

6. The <u>high price of drugs</u> (is one factor) in the <u>rising cost</u>
   <u>of health care in the developing world.</u>
   *C ... → ... E*

7. <u>Some human diseases</u> (have been associated with)
   <u>chemicals in the environment</u>.
   *E ... ← ... C*

8. Two months ago, the <u>town's only hospital closed</u>
   <u>down</u>. This will (have a major impact) on <u>public health</u>
   <u>in the region</u>.
   *C ... → ... E*

### Skill Practice 2 *Page 24*

1. B → C → A
2. B → D → F → A → E → C

### Skill Practice 3 *Page 25*

1. attribute
2. bring about
3. responsible for
4. thanks to
5. contributed to
6. consequences
7. link
8. lead to

# Reading 3
## Medicine and Genetic Research

### Connecting to the Topic *Page 26*

Answers will vary.

### Previewing and Predicting *Page 26*

| PARA-GRAPH | PROG-RESS | PROB-LEMS | KEY WORDS |
|---|---|---|---|
| 1 | | ✓ | *serious diseases, birth defects* |
| 2 | ✓ | | *significant milestone* |
| 3 | | ✓ | *unfortunately, no treatment* |
| 4 | ✓ | | *conquering* |
| 5 | ✓ | | *treatments* |
| 6 | | ✓ | *problems and limitations* |
| 7 | ✓ | | *setbacks, pursue research* |
| 8 | ✓ | | *considerable progress* |
| 9 | ✓ | | *revived interest* |

### While You Read *Page 26*

1. It could become more difficult for patients with genetic conditions to obtain insurance.
2. b) The second sentence
3. However, three basic technical challenges stood in the way of their progress.
4. In the first years of the twenty-first century, positive results began to emerge, arousing renewed interest in the field.

# Reading Skill Development

## Main Idea Check  Page 30

A 7  D 8
B 4  E 3
C 1

## A Closer Look  Page 30

1. a
2. False
3. a, b, d
4. True
5. b
6. B → C → D → A

## Skill Review  Page 31

**A**

1. The early results seemed very encouraging and,
   $\overset{C}{}$ consequently, people with genetic diseases became
   $\overset{E}{}$
   hopeful that they would soon see a cure.
2. Sometimes the therapy caused more problems than it
   $\overset{C}{}$ solved.
   $\overset{E}{}$
3. In the case of the French children, it caused a type of
   $\overset{C}{}$ cancer in several of the children, one of whom died.
   $\overset{E}{}$

**B**

Unfortunately, for some genetic diseases, there is no treatment, which gives rise to even more complex ethical issues. Would patients want to know that they are going to die young or become very sick if there is no treatment? Some may want to know so that they can prepare themselves. If there is a chance they could pass the disease to their future children, they may decide not to have children. For others, however, the news could ruin their lives. They might prefer not to know about their condition and enjoy their lives while they are healthy, so they may decide not to get genetic tests at all. There are also potential negative consequences if this private health information becomes public. It could be more difficult for patients with genetic conditions to obtain insurance.

# Vocabulary Development

## Definitions  Page 32

1. defective
2. milestone
3. ethical
4. obtain
5. therapy
6. immune
7. underestimate
8. setback
9. emerge
10. potential

## Word Families  Page 32

1. pursue
2. achievement
3. revive
4. inherited
5. pursuit
6. conquered
7. achieve
8. inheritance
9. conquest
10. revival

# Reading 4
## Malaria: Portrait of a Disease

## Connecting to the Topic  Page 34

Answers will vary.

## Previewing and Predicting  Page 34

A, B, C, F, G

## While You Read  Page 34

1. eliminating the places where they lay their eggs and killing the mature insects
2. The mosquito population can be controlled by spraying insecticide indoors, where people live and sleep
3. The problem is that in areas where malaria is the most prevalent, many people have little or no access to health care, so early diagnosis and treatment are often not possible.
4. One study estimated that in countries that are heavily affected, malaria is responsible for a 1.3 percent reduction in economic growth every year.

# Reading Skill Development

## Main Idea Check  Page 39

A 9  D 10
B 5  E 6
C 3

## A Closer Look  Page 39

1. b
2. b, c, d
3. b, d, e
4. False
5. False
6. b

## Skill Review  *Page 40*

**A**

3.    Malaria is spread by mosquitoes, which are host to the parasites that cause the disease. Just one mosquito bite can lead to a malaria infection. When a mosquito bites a person with malaria, it draws blood filled with parasites. The parasites continue to multiply inside the mosquito. Later, when the mosquito bites a healthy person, it introduces parasites into that person's blood. In one week or up to several months after the mosquito bite, the person may develop symptoms of malaria, including fever, headache, vomiting, and extreme fatigue. Not everyone who is bitten develops malaria, and people who have had the disease develop some level of immunity. Children, pregnant women, and travelers without any immunity are the most vulnerable to the disease. Eighty-five percent of all malaria deaths are children who are younger than five.

4.    The spread of malaria can usually be attributed to two features of the environment. It is most likely to spread in conditions where lots of people live close together and where mosquitoes can live and breed. Mosquitoes thrive in warm, wet climates, and most of them lay their eggs in standing water. The best way to stop the spread of malaria is to prevent it. The first line of defense in malaria prevention is eradication of the mosquito population. There are two strategies for eradicating mosquitoes: eliminating the places where they lay their eggs, and killing the mature insects. The first strategy is relatively straightforward. Even small pools of standing water, for example, pots that collect rainwater, can become breeding grounds for mosquitoes. Elimination of all of these pools can bring about a significant reduction in the number of mosquitoes.

5.    The second eradication strategy is more complicated. The mosquito population can be controlled by spraying insecticide indoors, where people live and sleep. After the walls of a home have been sprayed with insecticide, mosquitoes that land on these walls will die. However, the spray is not effective for very long, so homes must be sprayed every three to six months to maintain effectiveness. In addition, insects can develop resistance to these insecticides so they are no longer effective, eventually requiring stronger and stronger chemicals, which may have other serious negative effects on health.

6.    The next line of defense is to stop the mosquitoes from biting people. Because mosquitoes bite mostly at night, sleeping under a net can offer protection. Treating the nets with insecticides significantly enhances their effectiveness. All of these are relatively inexpensive measures, yet even they are out of reach of the poorest populations. As a result, in spite of the fact that these methods of malaria prevention are well known and available, an estimated 216 million people contracted the disease in 2010, according to the World Malaria Report. Like many diseases, malaria disproportionately affects the poor, especially those who live in remote, rural areas. (See Figure 1.)

7.    Treating malaria is more difficult and more expensive than preventing it, but early diagnosis and treatment are major factors in a patient's chances of recovery. The problem is that in areas where malaria is the most prevalent, many people have little or no access to healthcare, so early diagnosis and treatment are often not possible. There are several types of effective treatment, but again, the problem is access and cost. From some villages, it can take a day of travel on bad roads to reach the nearest clinic. Furthermore, the parasites are beginning to develop resistance to some of the medicines that have been used to treat malaria.

**B, C**

$$C \rightarrow A \rightarrow D \rightarrow B$$
$$\uparrow \quad \uparrow \quad \uparrow \quad \uparrow$$
$$F \quad G \quad H \quad E$$

# Vocabulary Development

## Definitions  *Page 41*

| | |
|---|---|
| 1. transmit | 9. insecticide |
| 2. leading | 10. disproportionately |
| 3. pervade | 11. philanthropic |
| 4. host | 12. linger |
| 5. parasite | 13. cognitive |
| 6. vulnerable | 14. impairment |
| 7. breed | 15. perpetuate |
| 8. spray | |

## Synonyms  *Page 41*

| | |
|---|---|
| 1. reluctant | 6. fatigue |
| 2. primarily | 7. rural |
| 3. straightforward | 8. preliminary |
| 4. thrive | 9. depressed |
| 5. enhance | 10. remote |

## Academic Word List  *Page 42*

| | |
|---|---|
| 1. transmit | 6. emerged |
| 2. ethical | 7. primarily |
| 3. underestimated | 8. preliminary |
| 4. achievements | 9. obtain |
| 5. enhances | 10. reluctant |

# Skills and Strategies 3
## Managing Unknown Vocabulary

### Skill Practice 1 *Page 45*

2. B foods with animal fat, such as meat, eggs, and cheese.
3. A
4. B less serious
5. A
6. A
7. B these ongoing efforts
8. B care from a doctor

### Skill Practice 2 *Page 46*

| STRATEGY | 1 | 2 | 3 | 4 | 5 | 6 | 7 | 8 |
|---|---|---|---|---|---|---|---|---|
| A definition | ✓ | | | | | | | |
| A contrast | | | | ✓ | | | | |
| An example | | ✓ | | | | | | |
| Other words or context clues | ✓ | | | | | | ✓ | ✓ |
| Similar to a familiar word | | | | | | | | |

### Skill Practice 3 *Page 46*

2. find out what is wrong with
3. became worse
4. large occurrence of an infectious disease
5. death
6. poisonous

# Reading 5
## The Health Care Divide

### Connecting to the Topic *Page 47*

Answers will vary.

### Previewing and Predicting *Page 47*

| SECTION | TOPIC |
|---|---|
| *III* | Problems related to getting good health care |
| *I* | Worldwide recognition of the importance of good health care |
| *IV* | Financial concerns related to health care |
| *II* | Various illnesses that countries are fighting |
| *V* | Health-care challenges and the future |

### While You Read *Page 47*

1. diseases, cholera, typhoid, malaria
2. Consequently, b) Effect
3. In addition to infectious diseases, a new global health threat has emerged in the past century: noncommunicable diseases (NCDs), such as heart disease, cancer, and diabetes.
4. b) No
5. Almost 300,000 women die each year – about 1,000 a day – from causes related to pregnancy and childbirth, and 99 percent of those deaths occur in the poorest, most remote areas of the developing world; for Sub-Saharan women, the risk of death before, during, or shortly after childbirth is 1 in 22 compared with 1 in 7,300 in developed regions, where a skilled health-care worker is present at almost every birth.
6. results in; understaffing of health-care facilities; reduces the number of medical school professors to train doctors for the future in the developing world
7. older people usually have more serious medical problems than younger people
8. significantly less money to spend on health care; many developing countries spend less than $30 per person each year; find ways to cover the costs of fighting infectious diseases and to provide medical help for the increasing number of people with NCDs, as well
9. Highly priced medicines are also a problem in developed nations lacking universal health care, and they especially affect poor people.
10. Countries all over the world are also taking a big step forward with both high-tech and nontechnological solutions

# Reading Skill Development
## Main Idea Check *Page 54*

**Section II**
A 6
B 5
C 3

**Section III**
A 10
B 8
C 9

**Section IV**
A 13
B 12
C 14

**Section V**
A 19
B 16
C 17

## A Closer Look  *Page 54*

1. d
2. c
3. b
4. d
5. False
6. c
7. b, d
8. a, d

## Skill Review  *Page 56*

2. relating to mothers: **Maternal** mortality rates clearly demonstrate the consequences of such shortages. Almost 300,000 women die each year from causes related to pregnancy and childbirth, . . .

3. a kind of drug for people with diabetes: For instance, several developing countries have no or extremely limited stocks of **insulin**, a drug that many diabetics need to survive.

4. describes an illness that continues for a long time: NCDs tend to be serious **chronic** conditions, meaning that patients will have the conditions for a long period of time, thus requiring higher expenditures for their care.

5. using their own money: Since governments cannot often cover the costs of drugs, most people pay for them **out of pocket**, that is, with their own money.

6. enough: . . . that every nation train its own people and provide them with incentives to stay in the country. Over time, this will ensure that countries have **ample** national workforces.

# Vocabulary Development

## Definitions  *Page 57*

1. priority
2. commitment
3. evident
4. discrepancy
5. adequate
6. hinders
7. capacity
8. invested
9. efficiency
10. sacrifice
11. prohibitive
12. patent
13. incentives
14. implementing
15. expansion

## Words in Context  *Page 57*

1. d  (contaminated)
2. c  (ongoing)
3. b  (plague)
4. a  (critical)
5. i  (facilities)
6. h  (ensure)
7. j  (tend)
8. e  (expenditures)
9. g  (affordable)
10. f  (immense)

## Same or Different  *Page 58*

1. S
2. D
3. S
4. D
5. S
6. S
7. D
8. S

## Academic Word List  *Page 59*

1. project
2. facilities
3. pursue
4. potential
5. ensure
6. awareness
7. capacity
8. priority
9. outcome
10. expansion
11. implementing
12. disproportionately
13. conduct
14. demonstrate
15. commitment

# Making Connections

## Exercise 1  *Page 61*

1. c
2. b
3. a
4. b
5. a

## Exercise 2  *Page 61*

1. BCA
2. ACB
3. CAB
4. BAC
5. BCA

# 2 Multicultural Societies

## Skills and Strategies 4
### Continuing Ideas

### Skill Practice 1  *Page 65*

2. discovery
3. prediction
4. requirement
5. response
6. fact
7. opinion
8. decrease

### Skill Practice 2  *Page 66*

2. (This); thin rocky soil
3. (Such restrictions); immigration restrictions
4. (This demand); demand for labor
5. (This practice); prohibition of Chinese immigrants
6. (These policies); immigration policies that favor skilled workers

### Skill Practice 3  *Page 67*

1. changes
2. views
3. attempts
4. move
5. circumstances
6. attitude
7. statements
8. crisis

## Reading 1
### The Age of Immigration

### Connecting to the Topic  *Page 68*

Answers will vary.

### Previewing and Predicting  *Page 68*

A, B, D

### While You Read  *Page 68*

1. (b) to put into categories
2. The old agricultural system that depended on large numbers of unskilled workers was disintegrating and had left many farm workers unemployed. The farm work that remained available was difficult and uncertain. When a harvest failed, there was not enough to eat.
3. In contrast, life in the New World offered several pull factors that attracted immigrants.
4. strongest

## Reading Skill Development

### Main Idea Check  *Page 72*

A 4
B 6
C 7
D 3
E 5

### A Closer Look  *Page 72*

1. True
2. c
3. d
4. a
5. Canada, the United States, Brazil, Argentina
6. c
7. True

### Skill Review  *Page 73*

1. factors lay behind immigrants' decision to leave their home countries
2. between 1900 and World War I
3. the strongest demand for labor
4. the system of contract labor
5. physically demanding jobs

## Vocabulary Development

### Definitions  *Page 74*

1. hardship
2. transition
3. disintegrate
4. starvation
5. representative
6. recruit
7. stability
8. peaked
9. interest
10. demanding

### Synonyms  *Page 74*

1. subsequently
2. option
3. fueled
4. attractive
5. abolish
6. colossal
7. source
8. initially
9. persistent
10. endured

## Reading 2
### Who are Today's Immigrants?

### Connecting to the Topic  *Page 76*

Answers will vary.

## Previewing and Predicting  *Page 76*

| PARAGRAPH | TOPIC |
|-----------|-------|
| 5 | Illegal immigration |
| 3 | The reasons why people today choose to immigrate |
| 6 | Non-economic factors in immigration decisions |
| 4 | The economic needs of today's destination countries |
| 2 | The destinations of today's immigrants |

## While You Read  *Page 76*

1. Countries such as Russia and China, which have long been, and continue to be, significant source countries, are now also destination countries. There is also considerable mobility inside regions
2. Most people move to another country because they want a better life.
3. a large number of people also move across national borders illegally
4. family and community ties

# Reading Skill Development

## Main Idea Check  *Page 79*

A  5
B  2
C  6
D  3
E  4

## A Closer Look  *Page 79*

1. False
2. d
3. c
4. b
5. True
6. c
7. a, c, e

## Skill Review  *Page 80*

**A**

1. 200 million people
2. that immigration was in one direction
3. a better life

**B**

Answers will vary, but sample general words are:

1. factors . . .
2. achievements . . .
3. beliefs . . .

# Vocabulary Development

## Definitions  *Page 81*

1. swell
2. range
3. destination
4. former
5. essentially
6. consists of
7. financial
8. domestic
9. construction
10. authorities
11. status
12. minimum
13. wages
14. motivation
15. ties

## Words in Context  *Page 81*

1. a  unrest
   b  unstable
   c  take advantage of
   d  deport
   e  secure
2. f  contemporary
   g  mobility
   h  prospects
   i  the case
   j  unskilled

## Academic Word List  *Page 82*

1. minimum
2. range
3. motivation
4. Contemporary
5. transition
6. prospects
7. consist of
8. subsequently
9. options
10. source

# Skills and Strategies 5
Point of View

## Skill Practice 1  *Page 86*

2. The government would like you to believe that its programs are helping the economy to recover.
3. Most people who have not lived in cultures other than their own assume that the rules for polite speech and behavior are universal.
4. People who watch a great deal of television tend to perceive the world as more violent than it really is.
5. A frequent allegation that is made about people between the ages of 18 and 25 is that they have no interest in politics.
6. Using the latest statistics, which show an increase in the high school completion rates, the government claims that its programs have brought about improvements in education.
7. The tendency of immigrants to live in their own ethnic communities is sometimes interpreted as evidence that they do not wish to become integrated into U.S. society.

8. The researchers argue that much more information is needed before anyone can adequately describe how people adjust to life in a new culture.
9. Relations between the company and its workers worsened after the employees charged that the company wanted to destroy their union.
10. Among Americans, a common perception is that most immigrants enter the United States illegally.

## Skill Practice 2 *Page 86*

2. Some years ago, it was argued, usually by western experts, that overpopulation in developing nations was one of the main causes of widespread poverty. According to more recent studies, however, this analysis of the relationship between poverty and overpopulation is seriously flawed.
3. There is a tendency among nonexperts to regard primary health care in developing countries as exclusively for the prevention of disease. Yet a closer look at specific programs offers evidence to correct this common misperception.
4. The fact that some first-generation immigrants continue to speak their first languages might suggest that these immigrants and their families are unwilling to become a full part of their new society. Studies by social scientists, on the other hand, cast doubt on the validity of this conclusion.

## Skill Practice 3 *Page 87*

1. There is a widespread belief that cardiovascular disease is a problem only in affluent societies and that it attacks mostly men. This was perhaps true in the 1950s, when CVD was first identified as a major health risk. However, more recent studies indicate that this view of CVD is questionable. In many parts of the world, CVD is the leading cause of death among women under 65. It is also becoming more common in less affluent countries and is expected to become a leading cause of death.
2. Many people assume that the rules for polite social behavior are universal. They claim that all societies have the same rules, for example, for how and when to thank others. Yet research on intercultural communication shows that this apparently reasonable assumption is unjustified. In fact, the rules for social behavior may differ, sometimes widely, from culture to culture. Studies have established, for instance, that some Asian cultures do not give or expect to receive thanks while shopping, but Americans do.

3. Even before a measles vaccine became available, people in the west considered measles to be a relatively minor childhood disease that was more of an inconvenience than a danger to health. But past and present experience shows that such an optimistic view of this highly infectious disease is unwarranted. Measles, with its many complications – including diarrhea and pneumonia – is, in fact, potentially fatal. Before the vaccine became widely available late in the twentieth century, measles killed an estimated 8 million children annually. In 2000, the disease caused an estimated 700,000 deaths in developing countries.

# Reading 3
## The Meeting of Cultures

### Connecting to the Topic *Page 88*
Answers will vary.

### Previewing and Predicting *Page 88*
A, B, D, F

### While You Read *Page 88*
1. b) A feeling
2. adapt to the American way of life
3. the government believed that white South Africans were superior to black South Africans.
4. contrast marker: yet; view marker: suggest
5. view marker: argue; common view: poll results and votes against bilingual education are evidence of growing intolerance toward immigrants in Canada and the United States.

# Reading Skill Development

### Main Idea Check *Page 93*
A 5        D 3
B 9        E 4
C 6

### A Closer Look *Page 93*
1. d        5. c
2. b        6. c
3. a        7. a, c
4. False

### Skill Review *Page 94*

1. There was <u>widespread assumption</u> this was a necessary step in realizing the economic rewards of the American Dream.
2. Many people <u>claim</u> that there are advantages to the process of assimilation.
3. It can be <u>argued</u> that this sense of national identity has served the United States well for many years.
4. Another example is South Africa where, prior to 1994, The South African Government <u>believed</u> that white South Africans were superior to black South Africans.
5. Many people have come to <u>view</u> assimilation as a flawed process since it assumes that the dominant culture is superior.
6. Supporters of bilingual education <u>claim</u> that forcing immigrant children to learn all subjects in English causes them to fall behind in school.

# Vocabulary Development

## Definitions *Page 95*

| | |
|---|---|
| 1. interact | 6. embrace |
| 2. absorb | 7. tolerance |
| 3. merge | 8. core |
| 4. regardless | 9. opponents |
| 5. mainstream | 10. immersed |

## Words in Context *Page 95*

| | |
|---|---|
| 1. d  (metaphor) | 6. c  (severely) |
| 2. i  (poll) | 7. b  (dominant) |
| 3. a  (segregated) | 8. e  (innate) |
| 4. h  (unjustified) | 9. f  (harmony) |
| 5. j  (adapt) | 10. g  (classified) |

# Reading 4
## One World: One Culture?

## Connecting to the Topic *Page 97*

Answers will vary.

## Previewing and Predicting *Page 97*

A, C

### While You Read *Page 97*

1. c) The last
2. Indian by day, American by night
3. however; unreasonable
4. the media communicates ideas and values of the country of origin
5. c) The last

# Reading Skill Development

## Main Idea Check *Page 101*

| | |
|---|---|
| A 4 | D 3 |
| B 6 | E 7 |
| C 5 | |

## A Closer Look *Page 101*

| | |
|---|---|
| 1. b, c | 4. False |
| 2. d | 5. d |
| 3. b | 6. False |

## Skill Review *Page 102*

Answers will vary.

| TOPIC | COMMON POINT OF VIEW | OPPOSING POINT OF VIEW |
|---|---|---|
| The effect of globalization on cultures worldwide (Pars. 2 and 9) | Some sociologists believe that *cultural leveling will occur, that there will be one global, bland culture.* | Another point of view is *that as cultures interact, they will continue to change and adapt, but remain unique.* |
| The effect of globalization on India (Par. 5) | It is often argued that *globalization has brought significant advantages to India (strong economy; growing middle class).* | *The writer argues that this has come at a price (depression + quitting jobs in outsourcing centers).* |
| The exporting of American media (Par. 6) | The United States is accused of *cultural bullying, or pushing other cultures to accept American values.* | *The writer thinks this is unreasonable since demand for Western media has grown.* |
| American movies and television shows in France (Par. 7) | The French organizers of the competition objected to *a film that was connected to an American company.* | *The writer believes that the French support French films, but want the freedom to choose American shows.* |

# Vocabulary Development

## Definitions Page 103

1. vast
2. intricate
3. distribute
4. distinct
5. diminish
6. dismiss
7. erosion
8. icon
9. inappropriate
10. profound
11. relegate
12. prestigious
13. inevitably
14. values
15. countless

## Words in Context Page 103

1. bland
2. unfounded
3. static
4. alienated
5. profanity
6. brands
7. debating
8. dynamic
9. incrementally
10. influx

## Academic Word List Page 104

1. distinct
2. inevitably
3. erosion
4. inappropriate
5. distributed
6. adapt
7. interact
8. dynamic
9. unjustified
10. dominant

# Skills and Strategies 6
## Reduced Relative Clauses

## Skill Practice 1 Page 107

2. In the nineteenth century, Europeans wanting to immigrate to the United States could do so as long as they were not criminals and did not have any infectious disease.
3. Stories told by new immigrants indicate the challenges they face as new arrivals to an unfamiliar land.
4. In the nineteenth century, the economic hardship created by the transition from agricultural to industrial economies was a major reason for European immigration to the United States.
5. Acquiring an adequate knowledge of English is one of the first tasks facing many immigrants coming to the United States and Canada.
6. Most democratic nations with diverse populations have laws intended to protect ethnic and religious minorities from discrimination.
7. In the 1980s, a large proportion of the immigrants settling in Los Angeles were from developing countries troubled by poverty and high unemployment.

## Skill Practice 2 Page 107

2. Economic hardship caused many nineteenth-century Europeans wanting a better life to immigrate to the United States.
3. The frustration resulting from an inability to communicate easily and effectively is a common experience among newcomers to the United States.
4. Research showing evidence of how second and third generations of recent immigrant groups learn a second language suggests that their experience is similar to that of nineteenth-century groups.
5. A complaint sometimes directed at immigrants is that they are unwilling to assimilate – to become full members of U.S. society.
6. One experiment showed that adults applying for jobs in England were less likely to be successful if they had non-English sounding names.
7. The sacrifices made by first-generation immigrants to the United States were sometimes greater than any immediate benefits they experienced.

## Skill Practice 3 Page 108

2. Gene therapy may be able to help people who are suffering from Parkinson's disease.
3. Refugees who are forced to leave their native countries often find it a long and difficult process to become legal immigrants in a new land.
4. Under a law that was passed in 1980, refugees are no longer counted in the annual total of immigrants who are admitted to the United States.
5. The procedures that are outlined by the National Institutes of Health are intended to make sure that researchers follow the rules, which require them to report all negative side effects that are observed in clinical trials.

# Reading 5
## The Challenge of Diversity

## Connecting to the Topic Page 109

Answers will vary.

## Previewing and Predicting Page 109

A, B, C, E, G

### While You Read  *Page 109*

1. Discrimination generally increases in environments where the issues of cultural identity and economic security are at stake.
2. outsiders who arrive to establish new lives; cultural misunderstanding and the settlers' desire for land and other key natural resources
3. used by the miners
4. has resulted in; dispossession of their resources, inadequate social and economic support
5. In countries where the dominant population is white, people of African descent continue to suffer from the socioeconomic effects of discrimination.
6. b) Example; c) Contrast
7. view that in a secular country, religion should be a private matter
8. (c) advantageous
9. either b) or c) or both b) and c)
10. However; the weakness of this view; is that it does not take into account the long history of discrimination in the United States and its consequences. For example
11. (a) many
12. The government claims the tests will encourage more rapid integration of new immigrants
13. However; the research suggests that immigrants actually contribute to economic growth
14. a) The first

# Reading Skill Development

## Main Idea Check  *Page 116*

**Section II**

| A  6 | C  5 |
|------|------|
| B  4 |      |

**Section III**

| A  11 | C  10 |
|-------|-------|
| B  8  |       |

**Section IV**

| A  14 | C  13 |
|-------|-------|
| B  15 |       |

**Section V**

| A  17 | C  16 |
|-------|-------|
| B  19 |       |

## A Closer Look  *Page 116*

| 1. a, d | 5. a |
|---------|------|
| 2. d | 6. a, c |
| 3. True | 7. c |
| 4. b, d | 8. a |

### Skill Review  *Page 118*

1. Sociologists generally <u>define</u> prejudice as a set of irrational judgments about a certain group of people based only on their membership in that group.
   *Sociologists generally define prejudice as a set of irrational judgments about a certain group of people that are based only on their membership in that group.*
2. Although their pasts are markedly different, what all indigenous people share <u>is</u> a history characterized by disruption of their ways of life . . .
   *Although their pasts are markedly different, what all indigenous people share is a history that is characterized by disruption of their ways of life . . .*
3. There <u>are</u> over half a million Native Americans living throughout the United States today, and about one-third <u>live</u> on reservations.
   *There are over a half million Native Americans who live [or who are living] throughout the United States today, and about one-third live on reservations.*
4. The preferential policies currently being used in India <u>were</u> established largely to benefit the Dalit.
   *The preferential policies that are currently being used in India were established largely to benefit the Dalit.*
5. Quota systems, such as the policies favoring the Dalit, <u>are</u> illegal in the United States . . .
   *Quota systems, such as the policies that favor the Dalit, are illegal in the United States . . .*

# Vocabulary Development

## Definitions  *Page 119*

| 1. homogeneous | 9. stratification |
|----------------|-------------------|
| 2. bias | 10. merit |
| 3. massacred | 11. stringent |
| 4. impede | 12. cohesion |
| 5. integration | 13. allegation |
| 6. eviction | 14. compounded |
| 7. stereotypes | 15. sanctions |
| 8. secular | |

## Synonyms  *Page 119*

| 1. in favor of | 6. resistant |
|----------------|--------------|
| 2. banned | 7. remedy |
| 3. instituted | 8. contradict |
| 4. impending | 9. disruption |
| 5. irrational | 10. detrimental |

## Same or Different *Page 120*

1. D
2. S
3. D
4. D
5. S
6. S
7. D
8. S

## Academic Word List *Page 121*

1. financial
2. secure
3. instituted
4. bias
5. core
6. authorities
7. integration
8. construction
9. diminish
10. initially
11. stability
12. domestic
13. debating
14. contradict
15. persistent

# Making Connections

## Exercise 1 *Page 123*

1. c
2. a
3. b
4. a
5. c

## Exercise 2 *Page 123*

1. CAB
2. ACB
3. BCA
4. CBA
5. BAC

# 3 Aspects of Language

## Skills and Strategies 7
Identifying the Thesis of a Reading

### Skill Practice 1 *Page 127*
1. machine translation; c
2. signed languages; a

### Skill Practice 2 *Page 128*
**A**
1. language savants
   Claim: *Polyglots have brains that are special and different.*
2. men's and women's communication styles
   Claim: *The differences between men's and women's communication styles can cause misunderstandings.*

### Skill Practice 3 *Page 129*
**C**
Scientists say that it [Cryptophasia] is a fascinating topic but that the secret language can create problems for the children who use them.

## Reading 1
When Does Language Learning Begin?

### Connecting to the Topic *Page 130*
Answers will vary.

### Previewing and Predicting *Page 130*
A, D, E, F

### While You Read *Page 130*
1. b) The earliest stages of language learning
2. First, they recognize their mother's voice; second, they distinguish between language sounds and non-language sounds; and third, they differentiate between basic contours of their own language – the rhythm and tone patterns – and those of other languages. They can do all of these things within days of birth.
3. they have difficulty distinguishing between these two sounds; they hear them all simply as *t*.
4. or nerve cells
5. b) The earliest stages of language learning

## Reading Skill Development

### Main Idea Check *Page 134*
A 7      D 9
B 4      E 6
C 3

### A Closer Look *Page 134*
1. e           4. a, d
2. False       5. d
3. a, b, d     6. False

### Skill Review *Page 135*
Answers may vary but should resemble:
1. language learning of babies
2. Language learning begins very early.
3. Language learning begins as soon as exposure to language begins, long before babies speak.

## Vocabulary Development

### Definitions *Page 136*
1. extraordinary      6. utilized
2. prosperous         7. reproduce
3. fetuses            8. decipher
4. auditory           9. distinction
5. novel             10. sessions

### Word Families *Page 136*
1. retain             6. retention
2. acquired           7. Acquisition
3. exposure           8. accomplishment
4. perceive           9. perception
5. expose            10. accomplish

## Reading 2
Learning a Language as an Adult

### Connecting to the Topic *Page 138*
Answers will vary.

### Previewing and Predicting *Page 138*
A, D, E

## While You Read  *Page 138*

1. c) Age and language learning
2. The hypothesis states that if an animal or human does not receive the necessary stimulation during an appropriate period of development, it will not develop a specific ability.
3. or children who have grown up away from adults and civilization
4. c) Age and language learning

# Reading Skill Development

## Main Idea Check  *Page 142*

A  4            D  1
B  3            E  7
C  5

## A Closer Look  *Page 142*

1. b              4. a, c
2. d              5. True
3. False          6. c

## Skill Review  *Page 143*

**A**

1. Age and second language learning
2. Age of exposure is related to pronunciation
3. Second language speakers' pronunciation is related to the age at which they are first exposed to the L2.

**B**

| PARAGRAPH NUMBER | FUNCTION OF PARAGRAPH |
|---|---|
| 6 | Shows more specific application to *second* language learning |
| 4 | Provides scientific explanation for thesis |
| 3 | Shows broad application of thesis |
| 1 | Presents thesis |
| 7 | Discusses importance of main idea for teaching |
| 2 | Provides evidence for thesis |
| 5 | Shows specific application to language learning |

# Vocabulary Development

## Definitions  *Page 144*

1. conflicting          9. stimulation
2. dispute             10. visual
3. approximate         11. species
4. phenomenon         12. mastery
5. presumably          13. feral
6. catch up            14. abuse
7. overtake            15. precise
8. extends

## Words in Context  *Page 144*

1. a  Scholars         2. f  hypothesis
   b  fundamental         g  in the long run
   c  attain              h  superior
   d  proponents          i  counterexamples
   e  implications        j  observation

## Academic Word List  *Page 145*

1. approximate         6. utilize
2. Visual             7. Exposure
3. conflicting         8. attain
4. acquisition         9. distinctions
5. perceive           10. fundamental

# Skills and Strategies 8
Definition and Classification

## Skill Practice 1  *Page 148*

2. Primary school teachers often find that although their students have good decoding skills (i.e., they use their understanding of letter-sound relationships to correctly pronounce written words) this does not necessarily mean they understand the text.
3. An ethnic group can be defined as a group of people who share the same ancestry and culture and who often live as a minority in a larger society.
4. The family is the most important influence in teaching children how to interact with one another and to become members of society, a process known as socialization.
5. Geographers often use toponyms, in other words, place names, as important clues about the social, historical, and physical geography of a place.
6. Acquiring linguistic competence (i.e., the rules that govern grammar, vocabulary, and pronunciation of a language) is, of course an important part of second language learning, but it is also important to know how to adapt your speech to different social situations.

7. In the English language, intonation (i.e., changes in the tone or frequency of language) usually falls at the end of a sentence but rises at the end of a question.
8. Supporters of the whole language approach to teaching claim that students learn better by this approach than by phonics instruction, an approach that emphasizes teaching students how to sound out words.

## Skill Practice 2 *Page 149*

Possible answers.

2.  Linguists who study phonetics distinguish between two approaches to speech sounds. One approach is to focus on the way speech sounds are produced by the speaker. This is known as articulatory phonetics. A second approach is to study the way in which speech creates waves of pressure that move through the air. This field of research is called acoustic phonetics.

speech sounds
- way speech sounds are produced —— articulatory phonetics
- speech creates waves of pressure —— acoustic phonetics

3.  Status is usually defined by sociologists as the position of an individual in relation to other members of a group. Scientists distinguish two kinds of statuses. An individual has ascribed status, regardless of his or her abilities and wishes. This refers to being born male or female and being born into a social class or racial or ethnic group. Achieved status, the other category, refers to the social position an individual reaches through choice, ability, and competition.

status
- ascribed status
  - male or female
  - social class
  - ethnic group
- achieved status —— social position

4.  Psychologists studying motivation and its effects on achievement have identified two types of motivation. One kind is intrinsic motivation, the desire to perform a task successfully for its own sake. For example, answer these questions: Are you working hard in this class because you enjoy learning? If you had time, would you take more classes like this? If you answer "Yes" to these questions, then you are intrinsically motivated. The other type, extrinsic motivation, is the desire that results from outside incentives – the rewards or punishment that individuals may receive for doing or failing to do something. Are you working hard in this class to get a good grade or to be admitted to university so that you can get a good job later? If your answer to these questions is "Yes," then you are extrinsically motivated.

motivation
- intrinsic motivation —— perform task for its own sake
- extrinsic motivation —— the desire that results from outside incentives

## Skill Practice 3 *Page 149*

1. the way speech sounds are produced by the speaker
2. the way in which speech creates waves of pressure that move through the air
3. status, regardless of his or her abilities and wishes
4. the social position an individual reaches through choice, ability, and competition
5. the desire to perform a task successfully for its own sake
6. is the desire that results from outside incentives

# Reading 3
## Rules of Speaking

### Connecting to the Topic *Page 150*

Answers will vary.

### Previewing and Predicting *Page 150*

| PARAGRAPH | QUESTION |
|---|---|
| 4 | What is a *speech act*? |
| 2 | What is one explanation for miscommunication? |
| 6 | What knowledge is required for speaking appropriately? |
| 7 | What is the research evidence for cross-cultural differences in rules of speaking? |
| 5 | How do rules of speaking differ across cultures? |
| 3 | What are *rules of speaking*? |

### While You Read *Page 150*

1. the host is following a rule in her culture, which states that offers of more food are made once, or at most, twice. The student, on the other hand, applies a rule from his own culture, which states that you should never accept the first offer of food or even the second.
2. To perform them successfully, learners need two kinds of knowledge.

3. Once learners understand that a certain speech act is appropriate or even necessary, they must figure out how to perform it.
4. There is extensive empirical data supporting both the claim that these rules of speaking exist and that they often differ across cultures.

# Reading Skill Development

## Main Idea Check  *Page 154*

A  5
B  7
C  1
D  3
E  6

## A Closer Look  *Page 154*

1. d
2. False
3. b
4. b
5. c, d
6. a, d

## Skill Review  *Page 155*

**A**

These are rules that enable us to interact in socially and culturally appropriate ways.

A speech community is defined as a group of people who share both a language and rules of speaking.

Speech acts are actions that are performed by speaking.

**B**

Answers will vary but should be something like:
1. A speech act for saying you are sorry is referred to as an apology.
2. A promise is a speech act that tells someone you will definitely do something.
3. A complaint is defined as a speech act that says something is not good enough or you don't like it.
4. A refusal is a speech act that says you will not accept or do something.

# Vocabulary Development

## Definitions  *Page 156*

1. impression
2. interpreted
3. sincere
4. impose
5. transfer
6. compliments
7. call for
8. elaborate
9. excuse
10. minimize

## Synonyms  *Page 156*

1. conform
2. breakdown
3. empirical
4. modify
5. document
6. conventions
7. gratitude
8. unconsciously
9. hypothetical
10. govern

# Reading 4
## Languages in Contact

## Connecting to the Topic  *Page 158*

Answers will vary.

## Previewing and Predicting  *Page 158*

| SECTION | TOPIC |
|---------|-------|
| II | How multilingual communities are established |
| III | Why some languages disappear |
| IV | The role of the government in language use |
| II | Communities that use more than one language |
| IV | Suppression of minority languages |
| III | Economic factors in language use |

## While You Read  *Page 158*

1. is known as
2. second kind
3. many residents were eager to learn English in order to improve their economic situation
4. young people leave farms and villages in pursuit of better jobs
5. when children cease learning the community language and instead learn only the dominant language, the result is *language death*

# Reading Skill Development

## Main Idea Check  *Page 163*

A  8
B  5
C  3
D  9
E  6

## A Closer Look  *Page 163*

1. True
2. c
3. a, d, e
4. b
5. d

### Skill Review *Page 164*

**A**

1. After a while, <u>one language loses ground to the other</u> in a process known as *language shift*.
2. People in a community may choose to speak the dominant language, but <u>when children cease learning the community language and learn only the dominant language</u>, the result is called *language death*.

**B**

1. There are two main categories of rapid language contact.
2. a  colonial conquest
   b  migration

**C**

Answers will vary but will be something like:
**Classification statement:** There are two *main types of bilingual contact.*
**Definition 1:** *Stable bilingualism exists in a community for a long time.*
**Definition 2:** *In transitional bilingualism, speakers gradually change from using a minority language to the dominant language.*

# Vocabulary Development

### Definitions *Page 165*

| | |
|---|---|
| 1. policies | 9. maintain |
| 2. residents | 10. vibrant |
| 3. advantageous | 11. utility |
| 4. literate | 12. paramount |
| 5. administer | 13. cease |
| 6. sector | 14. dictator |
| 7. accelerate | 15. longevity |
| 8. gradual | |

### Words in Context *Page 165*

| | |
|---|---|
| 1. exhibited | 6. path |
| 2. contact | 7. suppressed |
| 3. lost ground to | 8. hastened |
| 4. coexisted | 9. vigorous |
| 5. vitality | 10. eventually |

### Academic Word List *Page 166*

| | |
|---|---|
| 1. modify | 6. utility |
| 2. sector | 7. interpret |
| 3. impose | 8. residents |
| 4. ceased | 9. hypothetical |
| 5. policy | 10. maintain |

# Skills and Strategies 9
## Passive Sentences

### Skill Practice 1 *Page 169*

1. Sociolinguists are interested in how languages vary. This variation is found in each of the three main components of language. It is visible in the lexicon (i.e., the vocabulary of a language); in its grammar (i.e., the rules which are used to form phrases and sentences); and in its phonology (i.e., the sounds of language and the rules that govern their pronunciation).

2. Research has also confirmed the existence of gender varieties, the English that is used by men and women. For example, in both British and American English, men tend to use the nonstandard pronunciation of *-in* of the *-ing* ending. They say "I'm eatin'" more often than women do, for example. Men also tend to use nonstandard grammar more often than women. The following is more likely to be spoken by a male: "I didn't see nothing."

3. In one final exam, students were shown exam questions the day before. University administrators admitted that mistakes were made and that security needed to be improved. They claimed, however, that the identity of the person or persons responsible for the cheating was unknown. They promised this would not happen again as all examination papers would be locked up until distributed at the time of the exam.

4. The language that is used by parents with two-year-olds has qualities that distinguish it from the speech used with older children and adults. Research has found, for example, that adults pronounce words more clearly when they are talking with children of around two. It has also been established that adults often repeat nouns rather than use pronouns.

5. How children acquire language has been a focus of study for many years. One theory was that children imitate, or copy, what they hear. Parents then praise children when they use correct vocabulary and grammatical structures and correct them when they make mistakes. This theory of language learning is known as the behaviorist theory. However, this theory has been disproven. Research has shown that children are not good imitators, and when their language is corrected by caregivers, children are often reluctant to repeat the model they are given.

## Skill Practice 2 *Page 170*

1. a
2. a
3. b
4. a
5. a

## Skill Practice 3 *Page 171*

2. For example, it is often considered impolite to ask about such things as salary or how much a house cost.
3. In some cases, students were accepted by the university, but a month later they were rejected.
4. This sleep debt is built up from weeks, even months, of lack of sleep.
5. The money had been illegally transferred to an unknown account, and it is likely that the government will be unable to recover the money.
6. Such assessments should be made by experts who are not working on these research projects and who have no financial interest in their success or failure.
7. Thirty-five percent of Europe's population in the fourteenth century were killed by Bubonic plague, a disease that fleas transmit from rats to people.

# Reading 5
## The Advantages of Multilingualism

### Connecting to the Topic *Page 172*

Answers will vary.

### Previewing and Predicting *Page 172*

| SECTION | TOPIC |
| --- | --- |
| II | Employment opportunities for people who know more than one language |
| III | The growing importance of Chinese on the Internet |
| IV | Going to school in more than one language |
| II | Economic benefits of knowing an additional language |
| V | Multilingualism and the brain |
| V | How multilingualism improves thinking |
| VI | How language is connected to culture |
| III | The importance of languages other than English |

### While You Read *Page 172*

1. knowledge of other languages was second on a list of the most desirable skills for job candidates, just after knowledge of information technology.
2. as a result of language deficits
3. English is more widely used than another other language on the Internet.

4. These students are sometimes referred to as "parachute kids" or "wild geese."
5. Subsequently, however, more sophisticated tests contradicted these results and showed that bilinguals reach the milestones of language development at about the same time as monolingual children. Analysis of the earlier tests revealed that that these tests were flawed because they were really a kind of language test.
6. They were better than the monolingual children at focusing their attention and ignoring distractions. In addition, they were better at paying attention to changes in their environment and using this information to solve complex problems. Furthermore, they were able to remember information about one task while they were working on another task.
7. a gradual loss of their memory and mental abilities.
8. Multilingualism is a resource for individuals, communities, businesses, and governments.

# Reading Skill Development
## Main Idea Check *Page 180*

**Section II**
A 4
B 3

**Section III**
A 6
B 7

**Section IV**
A 10
B 8

**Section V**
A 16
B 14

**Section VI**
A 17
B 18

## A Closer Look *Page 180*

1. c
2. b
3. a, b
4. True
5. a, c
6. b
7. 1 b, 2 c, 3 b, 4 a, 5 c, 6 a

## Skill Review *Page 182*
### A

1. Billions of people are connected through the Internet and cell phones.
2. The global markets are no longer limited by space, time, or international borders; . . .
3. English is more widely used than another other language on the Internet; however, its dominance . . .
4. . . . their decisions about their children's education are often informed by this understanding.

5. These students are sometimes referred to as "parachute kids" or "wild geese."
6. This belief was supported by data from tests of the cognitive abilities of bilingual and monolingual children . . .
7. The practical and cognitive advantages of knowing more than one language can be measured, but there are other advantages that may be harder to calculate.
8. For example, Chinese children in Canada might be encouraged to develop their knowledge of Mandarin rather than learn a new, additional language.

# Vocbulary Development

## Definitions *Page 183*

1. promote
2. consistently
3. isolation
4. candidates
5. boost
6. incidents
7. deficits
8. ideal
9. nannies
10. domain
11. ignore
12. distractions
13. anticipation
14. onset
15. heritage

## Words in Context *Page 183*

1. e (sophisticated)
2. g (seek out)
3. b (cue)
4. h (compensate)
5. i (bonds)
6. c (flawed)
7. a (personnel)
8. f (remedial)
9. j (flexibility)
10. d (socioeconomic status)

## Same or Different *Page 184*

1. S
2. D
3. S
4. S
5. D
6. S
7. D
8. D

## Academic Word List *Page 185*

1. isolation
2. ignore
3. Empirical
4. promote
5. implications
6. flexibility
7. documented
8. conventions
9. consistently
10. exhibited
11. anticipation
12. eventually
13. retain
14. conform
15. transferred

# Making Connections

## Exercise 1 *Page 187*

1. b
2. a
3. c
4. b
5. a

## Exercise 2 *Page 187*

1. BAC
2. BAC
3. ABC
4. CBA
5. BCA

## Skills and Strategies 10
Problem-Solution Texts

### Skill Practice 1 *Page 192*

2. When people move to another country, one obstacle they may face is <u>their inability to speak and understand the language of their new home</u>.
3. <u>Cholera and other communicable diseases</u> are a threat to the economies of many developing countries.
4. People who take multiple medications for several different conditions often experience complications when these <u>medications interact</u>.
5. <u>Toxic materials, such as chemicals, old computers, batteries, and waste from hospitals</u> present a danger to the communities where they are stored.
6. Many experts argue that <u>our excessive dependence on nonrenewable energy sources</u> is likely to lead to a new energy crisis in the near future.
7. <u>Human activity</u> continues to be a threat to biodiversity in some of the most fragile ecosystems in the world.
8. <u>Government regulations</u> can be an obstacle to the development of alternative energy sources and other emerging technology.

### Skill Practice 2 *Page 192*

1. One way to alleviate the burden of having large numbers of immigrants settle in one area of the country is to <u>offer them incentives to live elsewhere</u>.
2. <u>Increased support from the government for climate research</u> would improve our chances of stopping global warming.
3. <u>Ethnic communities</u> have been a source of support for new immigrants as they learn to cope with the challenges and hardships of life in the United States.
4. The United Nations is attempting to persuade the two countries to <u>begin tackling a</u> resolution of the environmental conflict between them.
5. Many countries in Sub-Saharan Africa are anticipating a severe water shortage in the coming decades, so government agencies are <u>making preparations to address</u> this issue.

### Skill Practice 3 *Page 193*

1. In most cities, roofs on buildings are covered with thick, black tar. Tar is inexpensive and effective in keeping out water, but it creates environmental (challenges): It absorbs an enormous amount of heat so that buildings with tar on their roofs become very hot in the summer. This leads to a need for constant air-conditioning, which uses a great deal of energy. One practical (remedy is) a roof garden. Recently, government buildings have been replacing their black tar roofs with roof gardens, which keep the buildings cooler and reduce energy costs.

2. The *tragedy of the commons* is a (dilemma) that results when competing interests continue to use a shared resource until that resource has been exhausted. Overfishing is an example of a tragedy of the commons. Overfishing has led to the collapse of several species of fish, such as cod, and the extinction of several others. In an attempt to (overcome) this (problem), <u>several governments and international organizations have imposed limits on the amount of fish that can be taken from the ocean every year</u>.

3. Many people think that the energy (crisis) is about oil and gas. However, in sub-Saharan Africa, there is another energy (crisis). People don't have oil or gas for cooking, so 70 percent of the people burn wood for cooking. Every day, they cut down trees for cooking fuel. This practice has led to widespread deforestation. As the trees disappear, the soil dries up and blows away, and crops fail. This leads to a constant threat of famine. One (solution) to this destructive cycle is <u>bamboo</u>. Bamboo is not a tree; it is a grass that grows quickly, sometimes as fast as a meter a day. In addition, it is renewable, unlike trees, which die when you cut off their branches. When bamboo is cut, it grows back and can be used again.

4.  Acid rain refers to rain (or snow) that has high
    levels of nitric and sulfuric acid. Acid rain causes
    many (problems) when it falls. It burns the leaves of
    the plants it touches; it sinks into the soil and makes
    it more difficult for plants to grow. It poisons lakes
    and rivers, resulting in the death of many fish. The
    (damage) to the forests causes (hardships) for the animals
    that depend on the plants for food and shelter, and the
    shortage of fish leads to problems for the animals that
    eat them. The primary cause of acid rain is the burning
    of fossil fuel by factories and cars. The only way to
    (deal with) this (problem) is to cut back on fossil fuel use.
    Alternative energy sources and hybrid cars can also
    help reduce the effects of acid rain.

# Reading 1
## Ecology, Overpopulation, and Economic Development

**Connecting to the Topic** *Page 194*

Answers will vary.

**Previewing and Predicting** *Page 194*

B, D, E

**While You Read** *Page 194*

1. threat
2. solution; remedy
3. a large proportion of the populations of developing
   countries consists of children; sharply decreasing
   birthrates can have a negative economic effect on a
   nation
4. b) The second
5. Today North Americans and Europeans are asking the
   people of developing nations to cease doing what they
   themselves did for centuries.

# Reading Skill Development

**Main Idea Check** *Page 199*

A  10        D  9
B  8         E  4
C  6

**A Closer Look** *Page 199*

1. c          4. b
2. d          5. a, c, d, e
3. D → C → A → B    6. True

**Skill Review** *Page 200*

| Problem | Problem |
|---|---|
| high percentage of children; therefore inevitable population will grow | not enough working adults; negative effect on economy |

| Solution |
|---|
| Controlling population growth |

# Vocabulary Development

**Definitions** *Page 201*

1. ecology          6. affluent
2. fertile          7. apparently
3. undernourished   8. exploitation
4. nutrients        9. irreversible
5. emissions        10. paradigm

**Words in Context** *Page 201*

1. vanished         6. obligation
2. sustainable      7. counter
3. emerging         8. reliant
4. Deforestation    9. negligible
5. catastrophic     10. interrupts

# Reading 2
## The Aral Sea: An Environmental Crisis

**Connecting to the Topic** *Page 203*

Answers will vary.

## Previewing and Predicting  *Page 203*

| PARAGRAPH | TOPIC |
|---|---|
| 7 | Solutions to the Aral Sea crisis |
| 5 | The environmental damage caused by agricultural development |
| 3 | The Soviet development of agriculture in this area |
| 6 | The effects of the environmental crisis on residents |
| 2 | Description of the Aral Sea in the 1960s |
| 4 | Short-term benefits of agricultural development |

## While You Read  *Page 203*

1. (general problem) ecological damage that results from poorly planned economic development; (example) Aral Sea region
2. a) The first
3. The Amu Darya river shrank drastically; this river was cut off from the Aral Sea. Moreover, the reduction in volume and water flow led to increased salinity. Native species of fish died out, and the commercial fishing industry collapsed.
4. To address the problem
5. crisis, problem; responses, tackle

# Reading Skill Development

## Main Idea Check  *Page 207*

A 4    D 6
B 1    E 8
C 5

## A Closer Look  *Page 207*

1. a, d    4. False
2. a     5. a, d
3. d     6. B → D → C → A → E

## Skill Review  *Page 208*

| PROBLEM | SOLUTION |
|---|---|
| Land in the Aral region was too dry to support extensive crop growing. | *Canals brought water from the river to the fields.* |
| *Environmental damage + human cost* | A conference of international scientists was organized in 1990. |
| a) *water levels were too low* <br> b) *salt levels in the water were too high* | A dam was built in 2005. |

# Vocabulary Development

## Definitions  *Page 209*

1. render    9. cope
2. mean    10. inhospitable
3. flow     11. saturated
4. volume    12. pesticides
5. marked    13. conference
6. receded    14. concluded
7. salinity    15. rebound
8. collapse

## Word Families  *Page 209*

1. irrigate    6. remind
2. intend     7. irrigation
3. transportation  8. transport
4. reminder    9. intentions
5. reversed    10. reversal

## Academic Word List  *Page 210*

1. collapsed    6. volume
2. exploitation    7. sustainable
3. reliant     8. concluded
4. conference    9. transport
5. paradigm    10. reversed

# Skills and Strategies 11
## Graphic Material

## Skill Practice 1  *Page 213*

Answers may vary slightly.
1. The price of oil fell sharply in 2008 from about $100 to around $60.
2. The high oil prediction assumes that demand from developing nations increases while demand from developed nations decreases.
3. If demand grows, the price of oil will be just under $200 by 2030.
4. India and China are predicted to have especially strong growth in the next few decades.
5. If demand does not increase, however, oil prices from 2013 to 2035 will remain approximately the same as they were in 2005.

### Skill Practice 2 *Page 214*

Answers may vary.
1. Emissions of $CO_2$ are increasing in developing countries, but decreasing in developed nations.
2. Seventeen percent of $CO_2$ emissions come from forest fires and deforestation. China is responsible for 23 percent of global emissions – now the world's largest emitter. Total global emissions have increased 16 times since 1900.
3. A growth in emissions reflects economic growth. For example, India, a growing developing nation, now accounts for 6 percent of total global emissions.
4. Twenty-three percent. If the economies grow, this percentage may increase but only slightly as these countries are trying to use more sustainable forms of energy.
5. China produces more $CO_2$ emissions than the United States and Canada combined.

# Reading 3
## Biodiversity and Tropical Rain Forests

### Connecting to the Topic *Page 216*

Answers will vary.

### Previewing and Predicting *Page 216*

A, C, E

### While You Read *Page 216*

1. b) China
2. are completely destroyed,
3. First, second, also
4. Para 8: forest reserves; Para 9: scientific research; Para 10: address the problems of poverty, international debt, and overpopulation
5. South America
6. continuing idea: such research; main idea: the pace of scientific research on tropical plant species needs to be accelerated.

# Reading Skill Development

### Main Idea Check *Page 221*

A 6
B 3
C 8
D 4
E 9

### A Closer Look *Page 221*

| | |
|---|---|
| 1. d | 4. False |
| 2. b | 5. a, c |
| 3. a, c | 6. d |

### Skill Review *Page 222*

| | |
|---|---|
| 1. True | 3. b |
| 2. d | 4. a |

# Vocabulary Development

### Definitions *Page 223*

| | |
|---|---|
| 1. unanimous | 6. generate |
| 2. extinction | 7. preserve |
| 3. botanists | 8. designate |
| 4. susceptible | 9. partnership |
| 5. properties | 10. conservation |

### Synonyms *Page 223*

| | |
|---|---|
| 1. substitute | 6. consensus |
| 2. combat | 7. debt |
| 3. harvest | 8. tackle |
| 4. catalog | 9. halted |
| 5. excessive | 10. renewable |

# Reading 4
## The Water Crisis

### Connecting to the Topic *Page 225*

Answers will vary.

### Previewing and Predicting *Page 225*

| PARAGRAPH | QUESTION |
|---|---|
| 5 | Which regions in the world face serious water shortages? |
| 4 | What do humans use water for? |
| 2 | How does geography affect water supply? |
| 6 | What is the financial effect of the water shortage? |
| 8 | What is the definition of a low-impact solution? |
| 7 | What are some general solutions to the water crisis? |
| 3 | How does human behavior affect access to water? |

## While You Read Page 225

1. c) unequal availability of water
2. a) Water-rich
3. 70%
4. than other people living in the same city
5. The Aswan High Dam in Egypt was built to irrigate thousands of acres of farmland. The Colorado River was dammed to provide water to California. China is investing $62 billion to pipe water from the Yangtze River to its dry cities and farmlands in the north. The desert-dry country of Saudi Arabia relies on the technology of desalination.

# Reading Skill Development

## Main Idea Check Page 230

A 8  D 7
B 3  E 4
C 6

## A Closer Look Page 230

1. a, d, e  4. b
2. b  5. False
3. c, d  6. a

## Skill Review Page 231

1. T  5. F
2. T  6. T
3. T  7. F
4. F  8. T

# Vocabulary Development

## Definitions Page 232

1. abundant  9. highlight
2. insufficient  10. runoff
3. atmospheric  11. thereby
4. topography  12. subsidize
5. periodic  13. purifies
6. strain  14. resolution
7. underlying  15. enforcement
8. costly

## Words in Context Page 232

1. a  rain shadow
   b  Prevailing winds
   c  moist
   d  traps
   e  precipitation
   f  staggering

2. g  converting
   h  filter
   i  exacerbate
   j  proximity to

## Academic Word List Page 233

1. underlying  6. subsidize
2. resolution  7. insufficient
3. enforcement  8. highlights
4. thereby  9. converted
5. generated  10. substitute

# Skills and Strategies 12
## Nominalization in Subjects

### Skill Practice 1 Page 236

2. The government's decision to raise income taxes has angered a lot of people.
3. The allegation by some people that immigrants take more out of the economy than they contribute to it is rejected by most economists.
4. The destruction of large sections of the tropical rain forest by multinational companies has led to protests by environmental groups.
5. The tendency of new immigrants to settle in their ethnic communities is sometimes wrongly cited as evidence that they do not wish to become integrated into American society.
6. The current loss of biodiversity due to the extinction of species is a threat to the health of the planet that will last for hundreds of years.

### Skill Practice 2 Page 237

2. The destruction of vast areas of the Amazon rain forest by wealthy cattle-farming businesses is driving large numbers of tropical species to extinction.
   *Wealthy cattle-farming businesses have destroyed vast areas of the Amazon rain forest. This is driving large number of tropical species to extinction.*
3. The government's decision to expand agriculture by using enormous amounts of water from the region's two main rivers for irrigation was the root cause of the environmental catastrophe in the Aral Sea basin.
   *The government decided to expand agriculture by using enormous amounts of water from the region's two main rivers for irrigation. This was the root cause of the environmental catastrophe in the Aral Sea basin.*
4. The public's lack of appreciation of the ecological and scientific value of rain forest species is an obstacle to solving the problem of biodiversity loss.
   *The public does not appreciate the ecological and scientific value of rain forest species. This is an obstacle to solving the problem of biodiversity loss.*

5. The clearing of forests by early human settlers to provide fuel, wood for construction, and fields for farming probably caused the first major threats to the natural environment.

*Early human settlers cleared forests to provide fuel, wood for construction, and fields for farming. This caused the first major threats to the natural environment.*

# Reading 5
## Climate Change: Managing the Global Greenhouse

### Connecting to the Topic  *Page 238*

Answers will vary.

### Previewing and Predicting  *Page 238*

| SECTION | TOPIC |
|---------|-------|
| V | The need to alter our activities in order to cope with global warming |
| III | Possible consequences of global warming |
| II | Certain gases have a warming effect on Earth |
| II | What we know about global warming |
| III | The warming of Earth is causing polar ice to melt |
| IV | Addressing the harm that global warming is likely to cause |

### While You Read  *Page 238*

1. consequences; Climate conditions around the world could change; alterations in wind and precipitation patterns; high frequency of extreme weather events, such as droughts, heat waves, and floods
2. b) 45%
3. these fossil fuels; coal, oil, and natural gas
4. concern; Atmospheric HFCs; the increasingly widespread use of air conditioners in the developing world, especially in India and China
5. b) 1940s
6. rain to evaporate faster than normal, drying vegetation. Dry trees and plants can then easily fuel fire; drought
7. damage / potential damage; take immediate steps to reduce greenhouse gas emissions; increasing energy conservation, replacing fossil fuels with alternative sources of energy, and preserving the world's forests
8. Environmentalists have identified several key energy-saving strategies.
9. carbon stored in trees; called *carbon offsets*

10. view, argue, claim; the initiative hurts people who depend on forest work for jobs, wood for energy, and cleared land for new farms and settlements.
11. b) The second
12. a) Context
13. However; *any two of the following*: the growing body of evidence makes it clear that the world cannot afford to ignore the threat of global warming; The long-term costs will certainly be even greater if we do nothing now; a "wait and see" approach is no longer tenable; addressing the state of the world's climate must be a collaborative effort and a top priority.

# Reading Skill Development

### Main Idea Check  *Page 247*

**Section II**
A 9          C 5
B 6

**Section III**
A 13         C 14
B 12

**Section IV**
A 18         C 23
B 20

**Section V**
A 25         C 24
B 26

### A Closer Look  *Page 247*

1. b
2. C → B ↘
   ↘      ↘ E
   D → A ↗
   ↗
   F
3. c
4. a, d
5. b, c
6. False
7. d
8. a, c

## Skill Review *Page 249*

1. . . . <u>the existence of global warming</u> is an unequivocal fact.
   *Global warming exists. This is an unequivocal fact.*

2. <u>The wide use of HFCs by manufacturers since the 1990s</u> was motivated by the need to replace the CFCs . . .
   *Manufacturers have used HFCs widely since the 1990s. This was motivated by the need to replace the CFCs.*

3. In recent years, <u>the accumulation of the heat-trapping greenhouse gases</u> has caused average global temperatures to rise at a much more rapid rate than in the past.
   *These heat-trapping greenhouse gases have accumulated. This has caused average global temperatures to rise at a much more rapid rate than in the past.*

4. <u>The melting of glaciers, ice caps, and large sections of the Greenland and Antarctic ice sheets</u> will also contribute to higher sea levels.
   *Glaciers, ice caps, and large sections of the Greenland and Antarctic ice sheets will melt. This will also contribute to higher sea levels.*

5. <u>The replacement of fossil fuels with clean, safe sources of renewable energy</u> would also be a highly effective way to reduce greenhouse gas emissions.
   *Fossil fuels could be replaced with clean, safe sources of renewable energy. This would also be a highly effective way to reduce greenhouse gas emissions.*

# Vocabulary Development

## Definitions *Page 250*

1. unequivocal
2. skeptics
3. greenhouse
4. unprecedented
5. threshold
6. ecosystems
7. submerged
8. unabated
9. landfills
10. hybrid
11. mitigation
12. protocol
13. imposition
14. conceivable
15. tenable

## Synonyms *Page 250*

1. contention
2. curb
3. undeniable
4. accumulation
5. pose
6. abandon
7. induce
8. adversely
9. substantial
10. attributable

## Same or Different *Page 251*

1. S
2. D
3. D
4. S
5. S
6. D
7. S
8. D

## Academic Word List *Page 252*

1. partnership
2. irreversible
3. pose
4. induce
5. protocol
6. periodic
7. attributable
8. unprecedented
9. consensus
10. abandon
11. reversal
12. accumulation
13. conceivable
14. imposition
15. emerging

# Making Connections

## Exercise 1 *Page 254*

1. c
2. b
3. c
4. b
5. a

## Exercise 2 *Page 254*

1. BAC
2. BAC
3. ABC
4. CBA
5. CAB

# Quizzes

# Reading Quiz • Unit 1

Read the passage. Then answer the questions that follow.

# Wearing Wireless

Doctors want their patients to make fewer visits to their offices. They also want them to stay out of the hospital. This is increasingly possible because of the promising new advances in wireless technology. It is now feasible to provide some forms of health care through small wireless devices that patients can wear. The market for these devices, often called *smart apparel*, is immense, and it is growing quickly. In 2011, about 14 million of these products were produced at a value of about $2 billion. Experts predict that by 2016, the figures will be closer to 200 million devices and $6 billion.   1

The first devices to be developed have been watches, bracelets, or other types of "jewelry." Their primary purpose has been to monitor a patient's basic health indicators, such as blood pressure, heart rate, and breathing rate. They can continuously transmit the information to a patient's doctor. This kind of information is very important because it can show whether patients are healthy and stable or if they might be heading for trouble. It is particularly valuable to patients with cardiovascular or respiratory diseases, who would have to visit their doctors frequently if they did not have these monitoring devices. Another important group of users is pregnant women. The devices can transmit information about their unborn babies to their doctors. This can help ensure that the babies remain healthy until they are born.   2

## The Latest Developments

More recent devices can monitor a much wider range of indicators. They can measure the level of sugar in a patient's blood, a patient's body temperature, and how much energy a patient is using. Like the earlier devices, they can transmit this information to the patient's doctors, who can assess it from their offices. In this way, doctors become aware of problems before the problems become a danger to the patients.   3

Now the developers of these devices want to go a step further. They want to offer devices that are actually wearable, that are part of a patient's clothing. This has been a considerable challenge. To ensure that the devices work effectively and provide ongoing service, the developers have had to solve two problems. First, they need to develop sensitive materials that can gather information continuously. Second, the power source has to be small enough to be wearable, and strong enough to be washable. Scientists have begun developing special fabrics that respond to body temperature and can gather information from the surface of the skin. Others have been working on batteries that are so small and flexible that they can be woven into cloth. These newest devices will not feel like technology; they will feel like a shirt or a sweater.   4

Monitoring health is just one of the purposes of this new smart apparel. Some will also deliver therapy to patients. This technology is like the patches that people use when they are trying to stop smoking. The clothing will continuously deliver small amounts of medicine through the skin. One day in the future, you may wear prescription jeans!   5

Wearable wireless health-care devices like these will allow many patients to live more independent lives. In the past, they may have had to stay in hospitals or see their doctors frequently. The devices will allow doctors to provide remote care, so patients can stay in   6 their own homes even if they live alone. The information from the devices will inform doctors quickly if there is a problem, often before the patients themselves are aware that anything is amiss.

## Wearable Wireless Devices for the Healthy

   Although the motivation for the development of these devices comes primarily from    7
concerns about patient care, industry experts say that the greatest potential for this market is not for people who are sick but for people who are well.

   People in developed countries are increasingly concerned about staying in good health.    8
They are careful about their diet, they exercise, and they try to control stress in their lives. Wireless apparel can help them manage all of these things. There are several devices already on the market—from bracelets to underwear—that can provide users with basic health information, such as body temperature, heart rate, and blood pressure. In addition, these devices can report how many steps a user takes, how many calories the user has burned, and even if the user is sitting up straight. For both the sick and the healthy, smart apparel may be in their future.

## A Main Idea Check

1. What is the main idea of the whole reading? (5 points)
    a. Soon you will be able to wear your medicine.
    b. New smart apparel helps people monitor their health.
    c. Wearable wireless devices make health care more convenient.

2. Match each paragraph main idea below to a paragraph from the reading. Write the number of the paragraph on the blank line. (5 points)

    _____ In the future, smart apparel will be able to deliver medication.

    _____ Doctors can get information wirelessly, allowing patients to live more independent lives.

    _____ Early devices focused on pregnant women and people with serious diseases.

    _____ Inserting the monitoring devices into clothing presents two challenges for designers.

## B A Closer Look

**Look back at the reading to answer the following questions.** (2 points each)

1. How many wearable devices do experts predict will be sold in 2016?
    a. 14 million
    b. 6 billion
    c. 200 million

2. Choose two items below to complete the sentence.
    *The first devices were designed to monitor _____ and _____.*
    a. blood sugar                    c. heart rate
    b. blood pressure                 d. temperature

*Reading Quiz • Unit 1  (continued)*

3. Today patients can buy clothes that deliver medication. **True or False?**

4. Doctors can receive health information from these monitoring devices. Why is this a big advantage over a visit to the doctor?

    a. It is a less expensive way for a doctor to diagnose health problems.

    b. Patients don't have to go to an office where a lot of sick people are.

    c. The doctor can diagnose health problems before the patient is aware of them.

5. What is one major challenge that smart apparel designers face?

    a. The power source must be part of the clothing.

    b. The technology is still too expensive.

    c. Many people are afraid to wear these devices.

6. Experts believe that the sales of smart apparel will be higher for healthy people than for patients. **True or False?**

7. Choose two items below to complete the sentence.

    *Newer wearable devices can also monitor the _____ and the _____.*

    a. number of steps taken          c. number of calories used

    b. skin temperature               d. breathing rate

## C Definitions

**Find words in the reading that can complete the following definitions.** (2 points each)

1. _____ is anything that you wear, such as clothing or jewelry. (*n*) Par. 1

2. If something is _____, it is possible. It can be done. (*adj*) Par. 1

3. A/An _____ is a small machine that has a specific purpose. (*n*) Par. 1

4. If something is _____, it can detect or be influenced by small changes. (*adj*) Par. 4

5. _____ is cloth or woven material. (*n*) Par. 4

6. A/An _____ is a note that a doctor writes to tell a pharmacy what medicine a patient needs. (*n*) Par. 5

7. If something is _____, it is not right or what was expected. (*adv*) Par. 6

8. A/An _____ is a unit that measures how much energy a food provides. (*n*) Par. 8

# Vocabulary Quiz · Unit 1

**A** The words in the box are words that you studied in Unit 1. Choose the best word to complete each sentence. You will not use all the words. (2 points each)

| | | | | |
|---|---|---|---|---|
| collaborated | conduct | discrepancy | eliminate | fatigue |
| inherited | invested | leading | link | obesity |
| prevalent | pursuit | revive | sacrifices | thrive |

1. Cardiovascular disease (CVD) is the _____ cause of death in the developed world. The second most common cause of death is cancer.

2. Two research teams _____ on the design of a low-cost, high-capacity water purification system. They worked side by side for six months.

3. The _____ between smoking and lung cancer has been well established.

4. _____, which is responsible for the rising rates of diabetes and CVD, has become a major health problem in the developed world.

5. Gene testing can help detect diseases based on traits that have been _____ from parents or grandparents.

6. Mosquitoes _____ in wetlands and in areas where water has collected, since this is where they breed and lay their eggs.

7. The patient was told to _____ fatty foods from her diet.

8. The hospital _____ in expensive new technology that was able to diagnose early stages of certain forms of cancer.

9. In order to pay for their daughter's specialized medical treatment, the parents had to make great _____, including selling their home.

10. Symptoms of the flu include muscle ache and fever. In addition, the extreme _____ that usually accompanies the illness makes it difficult to get out of bed.

**B** Circle the letter of the best word to complete each sentence. The answer is always an Academic Word List word from the unit. (2 points each)

1. The _____ results of the study are very promising; however, it is clear that more research still needs to be done.
   a. effective          b. preliminary          c. devastating          d. immense

2. Compared to just 25 years ago, there is now a much greater _____ of the risks of poor diet and a sedentary lifestyle.
   a. awareness          b. expansion          c. achievement          d. commitment

## *Vocabulary Quiz · Unit 1 (continued)*

3. The government cannot provide free health care for all its citizens because the cost would be _____.

   a. promising      b. defective      c. adequate      d. prohibitive

4. In the developing world, infectious diseases tend to _____ the very young and the elderly.

   a. breed      b. target      c. obtain      d. revive

5. Many fewer women would die during childbirth if healthcare were more _____ in developing countries.

   a. critical      b. accessible      c. ethical      d. cognitive

6. The number of deaths from malaria worldwide is _____ high among children under the age of five.

   a. virtually      b. primarily      c. contracting      d. disproportionately

7. Early _____ of the disease was key to its successful treatment.

   a. outcome      b. detection      c. impairment      d. pursuit

8. Health officials will _____ the drinking water to ensure it remains at safe levels.

   a. aim at      b. eradicate      c. implement      d. monitor

9. Check with your health-care provider before taking this medication, as there is a/an _____ for serious side effects.

   a. diagnosis      b. potential      c. disparity      d. indicator

10. The woman was _____ to have a genetic test done since, in any event, there was no treatment for the disease.

   a. reluctant      b. critical      c. key      d. tend

# Skills and Strategies Quiz · Unit 1

**The answers to the following questions come from information in Skills and Strategies 1–3.**
(2 points each)

1. There is always one sentence somewhere in a paragraph that contains the main idea of the paragraph. **True or False?**

2. Which of the following questions does a good reader ask when trying to figure out the main idea of a paragraph?
   a. How does this paragraph relate to the main idea of the whole reading?
   b. Which are the supporting details?
   c. What claim is the author making about the topic of the paragraph?
   d. How does this paragraph relate back to the main idea of the previous paragraph?

3. The last sentence of a paragraph is often important because _____.
   a. it often restates the main idea of the paragraph
   b. it usually repeats the topic of the paragraph
   c. it typically contains the most important supporting detail.
   d. it connects to the next paragraph

4. Cause-and-effect connectors can come either in the middle or beginning of a sentence. **True or False?**

5. Which of the following is not a cause-and-effect connector?
   a. *for this reason*       b. *nevertheless*       c. *so that*       d. *due to*

6. It is important to know cause-and-effect markers and connectors because _____.
   a. they will improve your general English language vocabulary knowledge
   b. they can help you find the writer's main ideas
   c. they signal supporting details
   d. academic writing often attempts to explain causes and effects

7. Complete these cause-and-effect verb phrases with the correct preposition.
   _____ 1. *to lead*          a. *for*
   _____ 2. *to be a factor*   b. *about*
   _____ 3. *to be responsible*   c. *to*
   _____ 4. *to bring*         d. *in*

8. Sometimes you should be satisfied with just getting an approximate understanding of a new word or phrase. **True or False?**

9. When should you skip unfamiliar words while reading?
   a. When they are long and difficult words
   b. When they are not essential for comprehension
   c. When they occur several times
   d. Always

10. Which of the following is not a strategy for managing unknown vocabulary while reading?
    a. looking for a definition          c. connecting to a word you already know
    b. using the dictionary              d. looking for a contrast

# *Reading Quiz · Unit 2*

Read the passage. Then answer the questions that follow.

# What is Diversity?

*Multiculturalism* can be defined as an attitude or policy that encourages and embraces a diverse society. But what does a diverse society look like? Very broadly, a diverse society or community includes many different kinds of people: men and women, old and young, rich and poor, as well as people of different racial and ethnic backgrounds.

One way to get a closer look at diversity is to examine a single community in detail. By some accounts, Queens, a county that is part of New York City, is one of the most diverse communities in the world. What does that mean? Different organizations and different people measure its diversity in different ways. The government usually measures diversity using the census figures. According to the 2010 census, 2.23 million people live in Queens, and there is no ethnic or racial majority. The most recent census figures indicate that about 28 percent of the people in Queens are white, 28 percent are Latino, 23 percent are Asian American, and 17 percent are African American. It is the most diverse of all 63 counties in the state of New York and also one of the least segregated. In other words, people of different backgrounds live together in the same neighborhoods, shop at the same stores, and attend the same schools.

### Another Level of Diversity: Culture and Language

What can explain this incredible diversity, which goes far beyond the basic census categories? Walk down the street and you will see the answer. You will find Mexican bakeries, Muslim butcher shops, and Chinese medicine stores, all in close proximity to one another. Queens has experienced a persistent influx of immigrants for more than a hundred years. City authorities estimate that today, almost half of the residents of Queens were born in another country. The largest number – about 13 percent – come from China; the second largest group – about 7 percent – come from Guyana. In total, the residents of Queens come from more than 100 different countries. Few other communities can match this level of cultural diversity.

This mix of people from all over the world inevitably adds another level of diversity – in language. City officials claim that at least 138 different languages are spoken in Queens. Among the most widely spoken are Spanish, Chinese, Korean, Russian, Tagalog, and Haitian Creole. Although more than half of the residents speak another language at home, most of them are able to interact in English as well. In Queens, you can even find languages that are disappearing in other parts of the world. In Queens, you are more likely to hear Vlashki than in Croatia and more likely to hear Ormuri than in Waziristan, where these languages were originally spoken. In some cases, these languages are only spoken by few people in the world, and some of them live in Queens.

### A Scientific View of Diversity

Diversity and multiculturalism are usually considered in social and economic terms, but the stunning diversity of Queens gave one scholar an idea for his scientific research. Spencer Wells is a scientist in charge of the Genographic Project, a research study that began in 2005. He and other scientists are using DNA analysis to try to learn about the origins of

## *Reading Quiz · Unit 2 (continued)*

early humans in Africa and to trace their journeys as they migrated around the world. By looking at the DNA of people alive today, Wells can follow the lineages of the human race. Every person's journey, from the origins of humanity, can be seen through their DNA. People have participated in the project by contributing DNA from cells from the inside of their cheeks. So far, more than half a million people have participated.

Wells had collected samples from people all over the world and traced their lineages back to their origins in Africa. He wondered whether it might be possible to find all of these major lineages where they cross in a single community, or perhaps even on a single street. He thought the best place to look would be a diverse community that has absorbed a large number of immigrants. That idea led him to Queens. He collected samples from almost 200 volunteers on one street in Queens and was able to find all but one genetic lineage in their DNA. The pathways from the origins of human life in Africa had led all over the world and in the end had come together again, in Queens, New York, one of the most diverse places on the planet.

6

## A Main Idea Check

1. What is the main idea of the whole reading? (5 points)

   a. Diversity can be found in DNA.
   b. People come to Queens, New York, from all over the world.
   c. Queens, New York, is diverse by several definitions.

2. Match each paragraph main idea below to a paragraph from the reading. Write the number of the paragraph on the blank line. (5 points)

   _____ A scientific project is tracing the migration throughout the world from its origins in Africa.

   _____ According to the 2010 census, Queens is ethnically and racially diverse.

   _____ Many different languages are spoken in Queens.

   _____ The source of much of diversity in Queens is the large number of immigrants who live there.

## B A Closer Look

Look back at the reading to answer the following questions. (2 points each)

1. What is multiculturalism?

   a. a community in which people come from many different cultures
   b. a positive attitude toward cultural diversity
   c. schools and neighborhoods that are not segregated

2. Choose two items below to complete the sentence.

   *The largest percentage of people in Queens is _____ or _____.*

   a. Latino                     c. African American
   b. immigrants                 d. white

## *Reading Quiz · Unit 2 (continued)*

3. Choose two items below to complete the sentence.
   *Two primary characteristics of this community are _____ are _____.*
   a. a low level of immigration     c. a high level of diversity
   b. a low level of crime     d. a low level of segregation

4. More than half of the residents of Queens are immigrants. **True or False?**

5. Which country is the largest number of immigrants to Queens from?
   a. Korea     b. Guyana     c. China

6. How have scientists traced the path of human migration?
   a. They find out the history of how people traveled from Africa.
   b. They analyze DNA from people all over the world.
   c. They collect blood samples from the world's population.

7. The residents of Queens represented almost all of human genetic lineages.
   **True or False?**

## C Definitions
**Find words in the reading that can complete the following definitions.** (2 points each)

1. A/an _____ is a report about something that happened. (*n*) Par. 2

2. The _____ is a government program that counts all of the people in the country. (*n*) Par. 2

3. A/an _____ is a number or amount. (*n*) Par. 2

4. To _____ something is to be equal to it. (*v*) Par. 3

5. A/an _____ fact is very surprising, even shocking. (*adj*) Par. 5

6. A/an _____ is all the living things that are related to some living thing from long ago. (*n*) Par. 5

7. To _____ something is to find out how it developed. (*v*) Par. 6

8. A/an _____ is someone who does work or contributes something without pay. (*n*) Par. 6

# Vocabulary Quiz · Unit 2

**A** The words in the box are words that you studied in Unit 2. Choose the best word to complete each sentence. You will not use all the words. (2 points each)

| | | | | |
|---|---|---|---|---|
| alienated | authorities | compound | domestic | dominant |
| financial | former | influx | initially | interest |
| profound | status | subsequently | unskilled | unstable |

1. Immigrants, even those who are well educated, often have to take low-paying jobs, jobs that are typically done by _____ laborers.

2. At first, the child felt shy and frightened in her new school, but she _____ adjusted to the new environment.

3. In the past, minority cultures eventually blended in with the _____ culture in the society.

4. The agency advertises jobs for _____ work in private homes. There are several openings currently for babysitters and housekeepers.

5. The school has a special program for immigrant children, which helps those who are feeling _____ and unaccepted by the other children in the school.

6. The company, like many others, outsourced its call center to India for _____ reasons; they could no longer afford the high cost of operating it locally.

7. While the _____ of the United States as a major world economy is still very high, countries such as China and Russia have been gaining strength in recent years.

8. The greatest _____ of European immigrants into the United States came at the beginning of the twentieth century.

9. With a/an _____ government, a food shortage, and no jobs, large numbers of people are leaving the country.

10. When going through security at the airport, you will need to show a photo ID and your boarding pass to the _____.

**B** Circle the letter of the best word to complete each sentence. The answer is always an Academic Word List word from the unit. (2 points each)

1. The Red Cross _____ food and clothes to victims of the tsunami.
   a. instituted      b. distributed      c. deported      d. classified

2. Going to a college in a foreign country is a big _____ for most young people.
   a. transition      b. peak      c. stability      d. destination

## *Vocabulary Quiz · Unit 2 (continued)*

3. In _____ Chinese society, young people graduating from college have opportunities that did not exist 25 years ago.

   a. detrimental      b. vast      c. stringent      d. contemporary

4. People often emigrate to wealthier countries so that their children can have more _____ futures than they themselves had.

   a. resistant      b. static      c. secure      d. bland

5. In the urban areas, there is a greater opportunity to _____ with people from many different cultures.

   a. interact      b. segregate      c. absorb      d. classify

6. This city offers food from almost every country in the world; the restaurant _____ are endless.

   a. disruptions      b. options      c. opponents      d. representative

7. When she was told that her new job would involve international travel, the _____ of traveling to other countries was very exciting.

   a. source      b. sanctions      c. prospect      d. cohesion

8. The Parliament plans to _____ the government's immigration policy and will hopefully come to an agreement that will satisfy all parties.

   a. relegate      b. debate      c. endure      d. diminish

9. Some officials argue that it is completely _____ to allow foreigners to work in the country but not give them resident status.

   a. irrational      b. secular      c. demanding      d. unstable

10. The airline's baggage department was courteous and tried to be helpful, yet despite their continued and _____ efforts to locate the passenger's lost luggage, the suitcase was never found.

   a. unstable      b. innate      c. core      d. persistent

# Skills and Strategies Quiz · Unit 2

**The answers to the following questions come from information in Skills and Strategies 4–6.**
(2 points each)

1. Which of the following is *not* a word that signals a continuing idea?

   a. *the*          b. *these*          c. *such*          d. *a*

2. A continuing idea marker is a word or phrase that _____.

   a. repeats an idea from a previous sentence
   b. anticipates an idea in a future sentence
   c. introduces a new supporting detail
   d. connects to the main idea of the whole reading

3. Match each general word with its function when it combines with a continuing idea marker.

   _____ 1. *claim*          a. for things that happen
   _____ 2. *practice*          b. for things that people do
   _____ 3. *reaction*          c. for things that people say or write
   _____ 4. *event*          d. for things that people think

4. View and assessment markers show a reader that the writer is expressing an opinion, not a fact. **True or False?**

5. Match each word to its marker type.

   _____ 1. *belief*          a. contrast marker
   _____ 2. *myth*          b. view marker
   _____ 3. *however*          c. assessment marker

6. The adjectives, *flawed, invalid, questionable*, and *unsound*, all describe opinions that the writer believes to be:

   a. accurate          b. weak          c. strong          d. ridiculous

7. Typically, when a writer writes about opinions, the writer expresses two opinions but does not indicate which one he or she favors. **True or False?**

8. Identify the verb in the following sentence that is part of a reduced relative clause.

   *Of the many immigrants pouring into the United States every year, some are coming because they have a relative who is living here and some are being hired to work in American companies.*

   a. pouring          b. coming          c. living          d. being

9. Writers use reduced relative clauses to add variety to their writing. **True or False?**

10. Change the reduced relative clause in the following sentence into a relative clause.

    *New employees are expected to follow the rules laid down in the company handbook.*

    a. that are being laid down          c. that have been laid down
    b. that lay down          d. that laid down

# Reading Quiz · Unit 3

Read the passage. Then answer the questions that follow.

# Rules for Conversation

Every day we participate in different forms of interaction. In some interactions, for     1
example, classes, meetings, or political debates, it may seem obvious that there are rules that
we all follow. Those rules tell us who speaks when or how you get a turn to speak. It may be
more surprising to learn that ordinary conversations also have rules.

## Taking Turns

Conversation is organized into turns. There are just two fundamental rules for turns in     2
conversation, and experts in this field say that these are followed fairly consistently across
cultures. First, in general, one person speaks at a time, without much overlap. Second, there
is very little silence between turns.

That sounds simple, but how do people know how to participate in the "conversation     3
game"? During conversation, people send each other subtle signals. The most important
signals come from speakers to indicate that they are finishing a turn. There are three
categories for these signals. First, speakers may make a visual signal, such as a gesture with
their hands or head. Second, the quality of their voice may change. For example, they may
begin to speak more softly, more slowly, or with a lower pitch before they stop speaking. All
of these are signals that the end of a turn is coming. Finally, and most important, is where
speakers look. While they are speaking, they usually glance occasionally at their listeners.
However, when they are about to finish, they tend to look their listeners directly in the eye.
All of these signals help listeners perceive the end of a turn so they can prepare to jump in
for their own turn. All of this happens unconsciously, without either person realizing what
is happening.

What do listeners do while they are waiting for their turn? They have several options.     4
They can signal their attention by looking at the speaker. They can also give what are known
as *minimal responses*, such as "mmm-hmm," or "yeah," which tell the speaker that the
other person is paying attention. Listeners who want a turn before the speaker has finished
often change the position of their bodies in an effort to get the speaker's attention. Or they
may simply start to speak while the other person is still talking. In other words, they may
interrupt the speaker. When this happens, the speaker has to decide whether to give up
the turn or to try to keep it. One way to maintain the turn is to keep speaking, perhaps at a
louder volume, and see if the person who is interrupting will give up. Because the rules of
conversation do not permit two people to speak at the same time for very long, eventually
one of them will stop speaking. In friendly conversations, people generally try to minimize
this competition for turns.

## Variations in Conversational Style

Although the rules of conversation are generally the same everywhere, there are     5
important differences across cultures, ages, classes, and genders. These differences
are generally of two types: (1) Silence: How much silence is permitted between turns?
(2) Overlap between speakers: How much is tolerated? In other words, how long can two
people speak at the same time? What happens when one person's rules are somewhat

different from another persons? What happens when the person you are talking to does not conform to your rules?

Consider this example: Imagine you are telling two of your friends a story about something that happened to you. They are listening and giving minimal responses, such as "mmm-hmm" and "wow!" You can see that they are interested in your story. Then one of your friends looks very excited and finishes your sentence at the same time that you are talking. Then he jumps into the conversation and says "Yeah, that is so interesting. Something like that happened to me!" Then he starts telling his own story before you have finished yours. You are offended because you have been interrupted. But he thinks the two of you are having a great conversation.                                        6

Scholars who study language use say that your friend is not trying to compete with you. For him, this is a form of conversational cooperation. By finishing your sentence and jumping in with his own story, he is trying to establish a bond with you. He is trying to show how much you share. Yet it is easy to see how breakdowns in conversation can occur and how one person can get the wrong impression. Learning about conversational styles can help you become more tolerant when you are talking to someone whose style is different from yours.                                                            7

## A Main Idea Check

1. What is the main idea of the whole reading? (5 points)
    a. There are general rules for the structure of conversation.
    b. There is variation in conversational interaction across cultures.
    c. Conversations are pretty much the same everywhere.

2. Match each paragraph main idea below to a paragraph from the reading. Write the number of the paragraph on the blank line. (5 points)

    _____ There are several ways that speakers can indicate they are finishing a turn.

    _____ There is some variation in conversations across cultures.

    _____ Interrupting another person's turn may cause offense.

    _____ All conversation follows basic rules for taking turns to talk.

## B A Closer Look
**Look back at the reading to answer the following questions.** (2 points each)

1. What is one of the basic rules of conversation?
    a. Don't speak when someone else is speaking.
    b. Give a signal when your turn is over.
    c. Pay attention to what the other person is saying.

2. Choose two items below to complete the sentence:
    *Two signals that indicate a turn is ending are _____ and _____.*
    a. minimal responses            c. slower speech
    b. a direct look at the listener     d. louder volume

*Reading Quiz · Unit 3 (continued)*

3. Most people are aware of the rules for conversation. **True or False?**

4. Choose two items below to complete the sentence.

   *Two ways to claim a turn for speaking are to _____ or to _____.*
   a. change positions                  c. raise a hand
   b. look at the speaker                d. start speaking

5. If someone interrupts you, how can you keep your turn?
   a. Speak faster.
   b. Speak louder.
   c. Change the position of your body.

6. Minimal responses indicate the listener is interested. **True or False?**

7. What happens when speakers do not follow rules for turn taking?
   a. They may not get a turn to speak.
   b. Other people are likely to interrupt them.
   c. They may offend other people.

## C Definitions
**Find words in the reading that can complete the following definitions.** (2 points each)

1. Something that is _____ is easy to notice and understand. (*n*) Par. 1

2. A/an _____ is the amount of time that one thing continues after something else has started. (*adj*) Par. 2

3. Something that is _____ requires careful attention to notice and understand. (*adj*) Par. 3

4. A/an _____ is a movement with the body, especially the hands, to show how a person feels. (*n*) Par. 3

5. _____ is how high or low a sound is on a musical scale. (*n*) Par. 3

6. To _____ means to look quickly at something or someone. (*v*) Par. 3

7. To _____ something means to allow it or accept it. (*v*) Par. 5

8. _____ means working together to achieve something that everyone wants. (*n*) Par. 7

# Vocabulary Quiz · Unit 3

**A** The words in the box are words that you studied in Unit 3. Choose the best word to complete each sentence. You will not use all the words. (2 points each)

| accelerate | anticipation | approximate | breakdown | cue |
|---|---|---|---|---|
| empirical | gratitude | ideal | implications | impose |
| mastery | perceive | phenomenon | promote | stimulation |

1. He stayed with his brother's family for three weeks when he first arrived in the country, but he didn't want to _____ on the family any longer.

2. Babies need a lot of visual and auditory _____ to best develop their language skills.

3. In _____ of getting a big contract in China, the company paid for all its managers to take a three-week intensive course in Mandarin.

4. Adults find it very difficult to _____ a difference between certain sounds in a foreign language if those sounds do not exist in their own language.

5. Although it seemed clear that there was a relationship between second language learning and age, it wasn't until researchers analyzed the _____ data that the hypothesis could be proven.

6. Even though both executives spoke some English, if the translator had not been present at the meeting, there would have been a serious _____ in communication.

7. The _____ number of English speakers in the world is 1.8 billion.

8. Before the company decides to sell off its foreign offices, the directors must first consider the negative _____ of such a sale for the employees and for the community.

9. Language shift is a/an _____ that occurs when two languages are in contact but one slowly dies out.

10. It is almost impossible for adult learners to achieve total _____ of a new language, especially its pronunciation.

**B** Circle the letter of the best word to complete each sentence. The answer is always an Academic Word List word from the unit. (2 points each)

1. There are several effective study techniques that can help with vocabulary _____.
   a. perception      b. domain      c. retention      d. onset

2. I don't remember the _____ moment when I heard I was accepted to the university, but I know I was very excited.
   a. precise      b. fundamental      c. vibrant      d. paramount

## *Vocabulary Quiz · Unit 3 (continued)*

3. Whereas children can learn more than one language perfectly, that ability is _____ lost as they grow into adulthood.

   a. unconsciously     b. eventually     c. presumably     d. consistently

4. If you refuse food that is offered at dinner in certain cultures, the host may _____ it as rudeness.

   a. cease     b. interpret     c. suppress     d. utilize

5. When using rules of speech, you must sometimes make a/an _____ between formal and informal situations.

   a. distinction     b. proponent     c. sector     d. path

6. The government is trying to establish a nationwide _____ for bilingual education.

   a. session     b. incident     c. policy     d. excuse

7. When speakers of regional languages live in relative _____, it is more likely that their languages will remain strong and not die out.

   a. isolation     b. exposure     c. heritage     d. distraction

8. In the future, knowing several languages is going to become more and more _____ in the job market.

   a. superior     b. hypothetical     c. sincere     d. advantageous

9. It is important to be _____ to many cultures and many languages in today's world.

   a. exposed     b. transferred     c. promoted     d. extended

10. If you only learn the spoken language in a new culture, but you _____ nonverbal signals, you might be misunderstood.

   a. contact     b. attain     c. seek out     d. ignore

# Skills and Strategies Quiz · Unit 3

**The answers to the following questions come from information in Skills and Strategies 7–9.**
(2 points each)

1. In academic readings, there is usually a statement that gives the writer's one central main idea or "thesis." **True or False?**

2. Where are you most likely to find the thesis statement?
   a. At the beginning of the first paragraph
   b. At the end of the introduction
   c. At different points in each paragraph
   d. In the conclusion

3. Complete the sentence with the correct words.

   *In a well-written academic reading, the _____ of every _____ should relate back to the writer's _____.*

   a. introduction       c. conclusion        e. main idea
   b. thesis             d. paragraph

4. When you see that a writer has used a technical term, you should expect the writer to also define it. **True or False?**

5. Which of the following is *not* a definition marker?
   a. in other words          c. to divide
   b. to be known as          d. i.e.

6. Which of the following is *not* a classification marker?
   a. category         b. reference         c. sort         d. group

7. The focus in a passive sentence is usually on the person doing an action rather than the action itself. **True or False?**

8. Which of the following is needed to form a passive?
   a. a form of the verb *to be*       c. a form of the verb *to do*
   b. a form of the verb *to have*     d. a form of the verb *to go*

9. What is the correct way to express the following sentence in the passive?
   *Russian is no longer the official language of the country.*
   a. Russian replaced the official language of the country.
   b. Russian is being replaced as the official language of the country.
   c. The official language of the country has been replaced by Russian.
   d. Russian has been replaced as the official language of the country.

10. Every passive sentence contains a past participle form of the verb. **True or False?**

# Reading Quiz · Unit 4

**Read the passage. Then answer the questions that follow.**

# Responsible Tourism

International tourism has exploded in the last 75 years. An unprecedented number of     1
people – almost a billion – travel every year for pleasure, and that number is expected to
increase. By some estimates, the tourism industry is the world's largest employer. It generates more than 5 percent of the world's gross domestic product. Many developing countries are reliant on tourism as a major source of foreign currency.

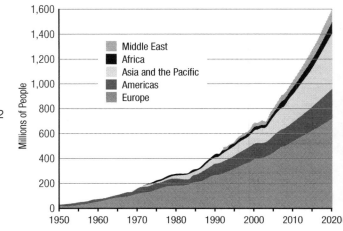

International Tourist Arrivals by Region (million)

Millions of People

- Middle East
- Africa
- Asia and the Pacific
- Americas
- Europe

*Source: International Trade Center*

## Negative Impact of Global Tourism

Some travel professionals have begun to pose     2
the question of whether this staggering number of international tourists is sustainable. This is a particularly important question for destinations with fragile ecosystems, such as islands, beaches, alpine forests, and polar areas. Can these areas cope with the rising number of tourists, or will it affect them adversely, in some cases, causing them irreversible damage?

Although many countries and individuals are eager for the economic benefits of     3
tourism, these questions highlight the fact that tourism can also have a negative social and environmental impact. In popular destinations, for example in coastal areas, locals may be forced to move from their homes to make space for the development of tourist services such as hotels and restaurants. In other destinations, such as the Serengeti National Park in eastern Africa, tourist development may attract locals looking for work. It can be difficult for these areas to support this level of human activity.

Most important, tourism often places an enormous strain on natural resources, especially     4
energy and water. In areas where such resources are already scarce, the high volume of tourists exacerbates the problem. Affluent tourists may use more water in a day than local people use in a month. The great temples of Angkor Wat in Cambodia are sinking because of the rising demand for water. Hotels and local authorities have had to drill deeper and deeper for water, and as a result, the water table is shrinking, pulling buildings down with it.

The problem is not limited to what tourists consume and take. It also includes what they     5
leave behind: waste. Cruise ships are popular in Caribbean destinations. They generate 82,000 tons of garbage every year, 3.5 kilograms of garbage for every person on the ship, and most of it ends up in the Caribbean Sea. This is more than three times the amount of waste generated by the people who live in the communities that the cruise ships visit. A similar picture emerges in the Himalayas, where thousands of mountain climbers discard plastic bottles, oxygen canisters, and food wrappers every year.

Studies of tourist behavior have shown that travelers who act responsibly at home may     6
forget their good habits when they are away from home. People who would never leave their

*Reading Quiz · Unit 4 (continued)*

air conditioners and lights on all day may do so in their hotel rooms. People who would
never toss a candy wrapper on the street in their hometown may do so on a dirty street in a
foreign city.

## A Code of Responsible Tourism

To counter this kind of behavior, tourism professionals and environmentalists have      7
proposed a code of responsible tourism:

1.  Responsible tourists have a low impact on the environment. This may mean that the
    number of tourists should be limited in some destinations. It may also restrict the kind
    of tourism in particular environments; for example, it may not be advisable to build
    large, high-rise hotels in some areas.
2.  Responsible tourists promote conservation of natural resources and the use of
    renewable energy. Sustainability should be built into development projects.
3.  Responsible tourists contribute to the local economy. This means using locally owned
    hotels, restaurants, and shops rather than large international chains.
4.  Responsible tourists try to minimize their own use of energy and resulting carbon
    emissions. For example, hotels have begun to request that their guests continue to
    use their towels and sheets for several days instead of requesting new ones every day.
    Responsible tourists choose public transportation rather than renting a car or hiring a
    private driver. Even small steps like these can make a difference.
5.  Responsible tourists leave the local environment as they found it. They stay
    on marked trails and they don't pick flowers or take anything out of its natural
    environment. They don't buy products made from endangered plants or animals.
6.  Responsible tourists show sensitivity to the local culture. They dress and behave
    respectfully in sacred places and during cultural activities.

By following a code of responsible tourism, both travelers and those in the travel      8
industry can help curb the adverse affects of global tourism and help preserve places of
natural beauty and cultural and historic importance.

## A Main Idea Check

1.  What is the main idea of the whole reading? (5 points)
    a.  Tourism is the world's largest industry.
    b.  Tourism often damages the environment and local culture.
    c.  Responsible travelers can reduce the negative impact of tourism.

2.  Match each paragraph main idea below to a paragraph from the reading. Write the
    number of the paragraph on the blank line. (5 points)

    _____ Tourists leave a lot of waste behind.

    _____ Tourists can take steps to reduce their negative impact.

    _____ Tourists use up a lot of resources.

    _____ Experts worry that an increasing number of international tourists may be causing
    permanent damage to the environment.

*Reading Quiz · Unit 4 (continued)*

## B  A Closer Look

**Look back at the reading to answer the following questions.** (2 points each)

1. There were almost a billion international tourists in 2010. **True or False?**

2. Choose two items below to complete the sentence.

   *In 2020, the largest number of tourists is predicted to come from _____ and _____.*

   a. Europe                       c. the Middle East
   b. the Americas                 d. Asia and the Pacific

3. What is an example of the negative social impact of tourism?

   a. Hotels use more water than people in the local community.
   b. Tourists throw garbage on the street.
   c. The construction of tourist facilities forces people to leave their communities.

4. Choose two items below to complete the sentence.

   *Two examples of the negative impact of tourism on the environment are _____ and _____.*

   a. overuse of scarce resources    c. large international hotels
   b. the large amount of waste      d. lots of cars

5. Why is Angkor Wat sinking?

   a. Flooding has caused many of the buildings to crumble.
   b. Buildings like hotels and restaurants are too heavy for the land.
   c. Tourists have increased the demand for water.

6. Experts suggest that there are some places that should not permit a lot of tourists. **True or False?**

7. What is the best advice for responsible tourists?

   a. Spend a lot of money in places that depend on tourism.
   b. Use resources like water and energy carefully.
   c. Stay away from fragile ecosystems.

## C  Definitions

**Find words in the reading that can complete the following definitions.** (2 points each)

1. _____ is the money used in a particular country. (*n*) Par. 1

2. Something that is _____ can easily be broken or destroyed. (*adj*) Par. 2

3. _____ means very, very large. (*adj*) Par. 4

4. To _____ is to dig or cut a hole in something. (*v*) Par. 4

5. If something _____, it gets smaller. (*v*) Par. 4

6. To _____ something is to eat it or use it up. (*v*) Par. 5

7. To _____ something is to throw it away. (*v*) Par. 5

8. To _____ means to throw. (*v*) Par. 6

# Vocabulary Quiz · Unit 4

**A** The words in the box are words that you studied in Unit 4. Choose the best word to complete each sentence. You will not use all the words. (2 points each)

| | | | | |
|---|---|---|---|---|
| costly | intention | negligible | obligation | partnership |
| receded | renewable | reversal | staggering | susceptible |
| sustainable | threshold | unanimous | unequivocal | vanished |

1. As responsible citizens, we all have a/an _____ to reuse and recycle.

2. The school board, in _____ with the local government, set up recycling centers on school property, and students volunteered their time to run them.

3. Americans throw out a/an _____ number of plastic water bottles: 60 million per day, 22 billion per year.

4. Although solar panels can be very _____ to install, the energy savings over time makes them worth the investment.

5. When the floodwaters _____ after the hurricane, residents of the area saw, for the first time, the massive destruction.

6. Weather forecasters had been predicting a heavy snowstorm for the weekend. However, in the end, the amount of snowfall was _____.

7. Our dependence on fossil fuels is increasing at a rate that is not _____, since oil reserves will one day be completely used up.

8. The town council passed the ruling in a/an _____ decision, and it was the first time that all the council members agreed.

9. I can't find my keys anywhere. They seem to have completely _____.

10. The scientific community is on the _____ of a major breakthrough in nanotechnology.

**B** Circle the letter of the best word to complete each sentence. The answer is always an Academic Word List word from the unit. (2 points each)

1. There's a growing _____ among scientists that climate change is real.
   a. intention     b. imposition     c. consensus     d. reminder

2. It took several decades to _____ the damage created by the oil spill.
   a. reverse     b. rebound     c. trap     d. render

3. There has been a movement to _____ nonrecyclable materials with recyclables in an effort to conserve natural resources.
   a. filter     b. convert     c. designate     d. substitute

## *Vocabulary Quiz · Unit 4 (continued)*

4. The move to encourage bicycle riding is going to face a challenge in the city because residents are so _____ on their cars.

   a. irreversible     b. reliant     c. undeniable     d. conceivable

5. Some people say that the wind farms _____ an unacceptable threat to the bird population.

   a. pose     b. preserve     c. tackle     d. induce

6. The city had to discontinue its research due to _____ funding.

   a. affluent     b. adversely     c. insufficient     d. emerging

7. After the investigation, the committee _____ that the oil company was at fault.

   a. reminded     b. generated     c. induced     d. concluded

8. The large amount of money raised for the victims of the earthquake was _____.

   a. saturated     b. marked     c. tenable     d. unprecedented

9. The government _____ the cost of the research that was carried out by the World Health Organization.

   a. intended     b. subsidized     c. abandoned     d. submerged

10. The residents complained to the city about the _____ of trash along the riverbank.

    a. mitigation     b. emission     c. resolution     d. accumulation

# Skills and Strategies Quiz · Unit 4

**The answers to the following questions come from information in Skills and Strategies 10–12.**
(2 points each)

1. How is a problem-solution text usually organized?
    a. First the writer describes a problem and then provides two or more causes of the problem.
    b. First the writer describes two problems and then offers one solution for both problems.
    c. First the writer describes a problem and then offers two or more possible solutions.
    d. First the writer describes a problem and then describes two or more results of that problem.

2. Which of the following is a solution marker?
    a. difficulty      b. setback      c. remedy      d. crisis

3. Which of the following is a problem marker?
    a. hardship      b. alleviate      c. deal with      d. resolve

4. If you see a problem marker, you are also likely to find some cause-and-effect analysis. **True or False?**

5. A writer rarely puts important information into a graph or chart; therefore, you can usually skip it while reading. **True or False?**

6. When you see such words as *See Figure 2.1,* _____.
    a. look for some statistics in the reading
    b. look for and study the graphic material
    c. continue reading to the end of the reading
    d. look back at what you have read so far and take notes

7. Match the names for different types of graphic material to the figures. Write the letters of the figures on the blank lines.

    _____ 1. A bar graph    a          b          c          d
    _____ 2. A pie chart
    _____ 3. A line graph
    _____ 4. A table

    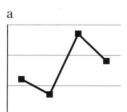 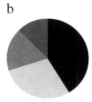 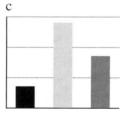 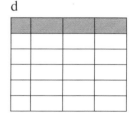

8. A complex noun phrase, or nominalization, can occur in different parts of a sentence. **True or False?**

9. Match the verbs to the endings that they take when they are nominalized.

    _____ 1. *conclude*      a. *-ation*
    _____ 2. *agree*      b. *-sion*
    _____ 3. *grow*      c. *-ment*
    _____ 4. *expect*      d. *-th*

10. If you have trouble understanding a sentence with a nominalized subject, you should try dividing the sentence into two simpler sentences. **True or False?**

# Quizzes Answer Key

# Unit 1

## Reading Quiz – Unit 1

**A Main Idea Check**
1. b          2. 5, 6, 2, 4

**B A Closer Look**
1. c          3. False        5. a          7. a, c
2. b, c       4. c            6. True

**C Definitions**
1. Apparel                    5. Fabric
2. feasible                   6. prescription
3. device                     7. amiss
4. sensitive                  8. calorie

## Vocabulary Quiz – Unit 1

**A**
1. leading                    6. thrive
2. collaborated               7. eliminate
3. link                       8. invested
4. Obesity                    9. sacrifices
5. inherited                  10. fatigue

**B**
1. b          4. b            7. b          10. a
2. a          5. b            8. d
3. d          6. d            9. b

## Skills and Strategies Quiz – Unit 1

1. False                      6. d
2. c                          7. 1. c; 2. d; 3. a; 4. b
3. a                          8. True
4. True                       9. b
5. b                          10. b

# Unit 2

## Reading Quiz – Unit 2

**A Main Idea Check**
1. c          2. 5, 2, 4, 3

**B A Closer Look**
1. b          3. c, d         5. c          7. True
2. a, d       4. False        6. b

**C Definitions**
1. account                    5. stunning
2. census                     6. lineage
3. figure                     7. trace
4. match                      8. volunteer

## Vocabulary Quiz – Unit 2

**A**
1. unskilled                  6. financial
2. subsequently               7. status
3. dominant                   8. influx
4. domestic                   9. unstable
5. alienated                  10. authorities

**B**
1. b          4. c            7. c          10. d
2. a          5. a            8. b
3. d          6. b            9. a

## Skills and Strategies Quiz – Unit 2

1. d                          6. b
2. a                          7. False
3. 1. c;  2. b;  3. d;  4. a   8. a
4. True                       9. True
5. 1. b, 2. c, 3. a           10. c

# Unit 3

## Reading Quiz – Unit 3

**A Main Idea Check**
1. a          2. 3, 5, 6, 2

**B A Closer Look**
1. a          3. False        5. b          7. c
2. b, c       4. a, d         6. True

**C Definitions**
1. obvious                    5. Pitch
2. overlap                    6. glance
3. subtle                     7. tolerate
4. gesture                    8. Cooperation

## Vocabulary Quiz – Unit 3

**A**
1. impose                     6. breakdown
2. stimulation                7. approximate
3. anticipation               8. implications
4. perceive                   9. phenomenon
5. empirical                  10. mastery

**B**
1. c          4. b            7. a          10. d
2. a          5. a            8. d
3. b          6. c            9. a

## Skills and Strategies Quiz – Unit 3

**1.** True       **4.** True       **7.** False       **10.** True
**2.** b          **5.** c          **8.** a
**3.** e, d, b    **6.** b          **9.** d

# Unit 4

## Reading Quiz – Unit 4

**A Main Idea Check**

**1.** c          **2.** 5, 7, 4, 2

**B A Closer Look**

**1.** True       **3.** c          **5.** c          **7.** b
**2.** a, d       **4.** a, b       **6.** True

**C Definitions**

**1.** Currency   **5.** shrinks
**2.** fragile    **6.** consume
**3.** Enormous   **7.** discard
**4.** drill      **8.** toss

## Vocabulary Quiz – Unit 4

**A**

**1.** obligation      **6.** negligible
**2.** partnership     **7.** sustainable
**3.** staggering      **8.** unanimous
**4.** costly          **9.** vanished
**5.** receded         **10.** threshold

**B**

**1.** c       **4.** b       **7.** d       **10.** d
**2.** a       **5.** a       **8.** d
**3.** d       **6.** c       **9.** b

## Skills and Strategies Quiz – Unit 4

**1.** c       **6.** b
**2.** c       **7.** 1. c;  2. b;  3. a;  4. d
**3.** a       **8.** True
**4.** True    **9.** 1. b;  2. c;  3. d;  4. a
**5.** False   **10.** True

Made in the USA
Middletown, DE
14 August 2018